The Index Card

The Index Card

WHY PERSONAL FINANCE DOESN'T HAVE TO BE COMPLICATED

Helaine Olen and Harold Pollack

PORTFOLIO / PENGUIN

PORTFOLIO / PENGUIN
An imprint of Penguin Random House LLC
375 Hudson Street
New York, New York 10014
penguin.com

ISBN 978-1-59184-768-7

Printed in the United States of America
1   3   5   7   9   10   8   6   4   2

Set in Minion Pro
Designed by Alissa Rose Theodor

This publication is designed to provide accurate and authoritative information in regard
to the subject matter covered. It is sold with the understanding that the publisher is not
engaged in rendering legal, accounting, or other professional services. If you require legal
advice or other expert assistance, you should seek the services of a competent professional.

To Veronica, Rebecca, Hannah, and Vincent
—Harold

To Matt, Jake, and Luke
—Helaine

CONTENTS

The Index Card

INTRODUCTION

SAM'S STORY

A few years ago, Sam received an inheritance after his dad died. Grief stricken and overwhelmed by the demands of work, marriage, and raising children, he placed the money in a local bank's savings account. Every so often, Sam would make an effort to think about the money. He knew he should invest it in . . . well, something. A few times a year a very official-sounding officer from the bank, someone called a wealth officer, would contact him about it, suggesting a complimentary meeting.

So Sam would sit down at the bank, and an advisor would offer him coffee and muffins and talk to him about his children, his job, and where he next planned to go on vacation. Then he would offer a solution, the next-best thing to a guarantee, he said, as he started talking really fast about expected rates of return, risk, and the importance of the stock market.

The wealth officer, or wealth specialist, or whatever the heck he was called, wanted Sam to sign papers right there and then so the money could get to work, as he put it. But Sam held off. He knew there were unscrupulous money people out there, and he wanted to do his due diligence.

So Sam would call friends, and friends of those friends. Sometimes those friends were in finance or married to people in finance, and they would make suggestions based on what they had picked up from their jobs or their husbands or wives over the years. One offered to manage the money for him altogether but didn't say how he would be compensated for his time and effort. Another said he should call Vanguard and put the money in something called index funds. Bonds, advised another. Others talked about allocating different percentages to different investments. Still another pal suggested a financial advisor named Kelly who had done amazing things for him.

Other people told Sam horror stories. There was the friend who had been persuaded to invest in tech stocks in 1999 and lost "a bundle," as he put it. A coworker told him about the friend of the family who seemed so kind but put her mom in some sort of investment that didn't do what it was supposed to and left her in a worse position than when she started out. Several people mentioned Bernie Madoff.

It was overwhelming. It seemed as if everyone contradicted one another. And they were all so sure . . . sure that they had the secret to how to make money grow or that it was all a rip-off. And Sam was scared. He needed that money. He wanted to send his children to college. He couldn't bring himself to risk losing it.

So Sam ended up doing . . . *nothing.*

Not only did Sam's nest egg end up losing a chunk of its value to inflation, but the stock market also did well during this period. Sam didn't benefit from that run-up. He wasn't running anywhere. He was stuck doing nothing because the combination of the myriad options and uncertainties of money, the economy, and the financial services industry had all but paralyzed him.

THE *POUND FOOLISH* STORY

Sam is hardly alone. Statistics and studies show that many of us choose not to deal or take a hands-on approach when it comes to our finances.

- Almost three out of four of us say our finances cause us stress on at least a monthly basis.

- One-third of those in relationships say money is a major source of conflict with their significant other.

- Fifty-five percent of people with investable assets worth between $50,000 and $250,000 say they fear outliving their retirement savings.

- Sixty-nine percent of us answered "never" when asked how often we balance our checking accounts.

The roller coaster that is our economy only makes us even more hesitant to take control of our financial lives. In her book *Pound Foolish: Exposing the Dark Side of the Personal Finance Industry,* Helaine told the story of how for all too many of us wages began to stagnate and fall, even as jobs and paychecks became less secure. At the same time, almost all the income and wealth gains since the end of the Great Recession have gone to the wealthiest.

We feel as if we are falling behind because, frankly, we are, often through no fault of our own.

We're convinced any financial mistake will send us on

a downward spiral we won't be able to recover from. Many of us walk around with a constant and growing sense that financial doom can arrive at any moment.

So like Sam we fret about our finances but remain frozen. Money feels complicated, boring, scary, and overwhelming all at once. Who wants to wade through competing budget apps? We want to be careful financial stewards but instead get caught up playing a losing game of financial Whac-A-Mole.

Desperate, we tell ourselves that someone out there must have the answer. All too many people working in the financial services industry market themselves as our friends who have special insights into the world of finance and future events. Even as we don't trust many of the financial types we encounter, we are secretly convinced there is one person out there, one honest man or woman, who can identify exactly that magic investment for us, and guarantee that our money will grow, and that nothing will go wrong, not ever.

But as *Pound Foolish* showed, many of our financial problems were not the result of our financial missteps. They were caused by economic trends and recessions and then compounded by the failure of financial regulators to crack down on bad behavior by those who claimed to be offering us help.

Many of *Pound Foolish*'s readers contacted Helaine to thank her for not laying all the blame of their financial woes on their shoulders, and just as many had a simple follow-up question: If we all need to be wary of the financial services industry, and yet we also need to be proactive about our finances, what do we do?

For a long time, Helaine had no answer to that question.

Fortunately, Harold did.

HAROLD'S STORY

Like Helaine, Harold does not work in the financial services industry. A professor at the University of Chicago and a contributor to a number of media outlets and blogs, including the *Washington Post*'s *Wonkblog*, Harold came up with the concept of the index card not as some academic experiment but as a practical solution to the kinds of urgent financial problems many of us encounter at some point in our lives. As he explains,

For most of my life, I had no real savings to speak of. I didn't even own a home until I was forty years old. My wife, Veronica, and I were not poor by any means, but we were starting a family. Like many people our age, we never displayed much financial forward thinking or savvy. I was putting money in my retirement account but basically treading water otherwise. We rented (and subsequently missed out on a historic real estate run-up). I invested in dot-com stocks. You can guess how well that ended. We had child-care expenses. We let some costly debts accumulate. We overpaid for a nice new car when a nice used model would have worked fine.

Then, as so often is the case, life happened.

Around the time of my forty-first birthday, Veronica lost her mother quite suddenly. Veronica's brother Vincent, who lives with an intellectual disability known as fragile X syndrome, was living with Veronica's mom. The issues were sad and complicated, but the bottom line was simple. After this untimely death, Vincent needed to move in with us and our two young daughters. Vincent moved in with us and our two young daughters.

Immediately, we felt the financial strain. Veronica had to leave the workforce to address Vincent's needs. Yet even as our income fell, our expenses mounted. And mounted. Vincent had multiple hospitalizations and medical challenges, many related to his morbid obesity. The La-Z-Boy chair we bought to support his 340-pound frame cost nearly $1,000. Not long after, Veronica developed a serious heart infection that landed her in the cardiac ICU. We weren't in financial free fall, but things were tight, and we were living a fundamentally different kind of life than we had ever expected.

I needed to quickly find some real answers to right our financial life.

I didn't have much financial knowledge. I did draw upon the tools of my academic trade to help guide me as I tried to distinguish the useful advice from the useless or worse. I consulted financial advisors and read books and academic papers on managing one's finances.

Through trial and error, conversations with friends and other academics, I slowly pieced together a new financial regimen. Some was common sense.

Some involved teaching myself insights that were actually well known to financial economists but underemphasized in the cacophony put out by the financial services industry. The most important advice was embarrassingly simple. It included the following:

- Save 10 to 20 percent of your money—or as much as you can, if you can't put that much aside.

- Pay your credit card balance in full every month.

- Invest in low-cost index funds.

By following these rules and a handful more, we saw our financial picture begin to brighten. Life didn't change overnight. But it did change. We had more money in the bank. We could afford to take a vacation without fearing what would become of us the next month if we encountered an unexpected home repair. We could exploit the various tax-advantaged savings offerings we could never use before. And putting money away allowed us to get lucky in the stock market; investment returns from the most recent bull market will help pay the college tuition for our daughters. We could refinance our mortgage on favorable terms. We found ourselves able to help out our relatives who were struggling. We felt financially secure, even though our house is still worth notably less than it was when we bought it in 2003.

THE INDEX CARD STORY

When *Pound Foolish* was published, Harold contacted Helaine and interviewed her on the *Reality-Based Community* blog. During their Internet chat, Harold offhandedly noted that the fundamental dilemma facing the financial services industry is that the correct advice for most people fits on a three-by-five-inch index card and is available for free at the library.

A surprising number of people wrote to Harold, asking for the card. Because he was speaking metaphorically, this was a problem. But he had promised. So he pulled one of his daughter's index cards out of her backpack, picked up a pen, and in maybe three minutes wrote down some of the simple and basic financial rules he and Veronica had been living by for the past decade. He then snapped a crude picture with his smartphone. This is what it looked like:

Max your 401(k) or equivalent employee contribution.
Buy inexpensive, well-diversified mutual funds such as well-chosen target-date funds.
Never buy or sell individual securities. The person on the other side of the table knows more than you do about their stuff
Save 20% of your money.
Pay your credit card balance in full every month.
Maximize tax-advantaged savings vehicles such as Roth, SEP, and 529 accounts.
Pay attention to fees. Avoid actively-managed funds
Make financial advisors commit to fiduciary standard.
Support social insurance for when things go wrong.

Harold posted the photograph on his blog, and things quickly went viral. There were hundreds of thousands of hits around the Internet. A life coach copied it word for word and read it aloud in a YouTube video. The card was even translated into Romanian. There were also shout-outs from people who have deep knowledge about personal finance, economics, and investments.

"Pollack's right. Follow these principles and you'll be in much, much, much better shape than most Americans—or most anyone," wrote Ezra Klein over at the *Washington Post*.

"Your new financial advisor is Harold Pollack's index card," declared the website *Boing Boing*.

Marketplace, Forbes, the *Huffington Post, Reddit,* and *Lifehacker* discussed it.

The MacArthur fellow Sendhil Mullainathan tweeted the card out. So did top economists like Justin Wolfers. Vanguard mentioned the index card on its blog and e-mailed a picture of it with accompanying information in a "Money-Whys" New Year's investment advice message to its subscribers. *Money* magazine called it one of the "best new money ideas" of 2013. The Minneapolis *Star Tribune* wrote, "The most notable personal finance writing of 2013 . . . was a handwritten 4 × 6 index card."

There were thousands of comments and tweets, Facebook likes, and LinkedIn shares. Among the index card's many fans? Helaine, who knew she finally had an answer for her readers. Rather than people relying on the so-called expert advice of the financial industry to dig them out of their money troubles and provide them with a magic bullet, she and Harold knew instinctively that the answer was much simpler and that it lay not with the experts but within ourselves.

One quick note: You'll notice we made a few alterations to the original index card. Most of these changes were either organizational or for wording, but a few are more significant. Most important: Harold originally suggested that people save 20 percent of their pretax income. It's a terrific goal. It's also all but impossible for many of us. Aiming for 10 to 20 percent is a more realistic long-term strategy. We also eliminated the recommendation to use target-date funds—read on to find out why. Finally, we felt it was important to include insurance and housing, both of which didn't make it onto the original card.

KEEP IT SIMPLE—THE ONLY STORY YOU NEED TO KNOW

So a question: If the rules are so simple, why do you need more than an index card—heck, a book—to explain them?

Most of us don't want to follow rules unless we know why they are rules. This book explains how the rules work and why we chose them. They may be simple, but they aren't always self-explanatory.

Simplicity—as anyone who has ever tried to perfect a golf swing knows—often takes work and insight to achieve. Just telling you financial rules to follow is not the same thing as showing you how to master them so that you can follow them with confidence. And you will need to because . . .

There is a whole industry of financial services advisors out there who make their living by convincing you that it's naive to believe that simplicity, common sense, and restraint are potent enough weapons with which to deal with the whirlwind of financial chaos facing any of us on any given day. They make their money by convincing you that investing is so complicated, you need to turn it over to them. Or they convince you that they—as insiders, as "professionals"—have the ability to outsmart everyone else and know exactly what investment scheme will outperform the S&P 500.

The financial world offers an odd juxtaposition. The financial products we use in our day-to-day lives—credit cards, mutual funds, mortgages—are often quite complicated. But that doesn't mean the way we lead our financial lives needs to be equally complicated.

Between Helaine's experience covering the pitfalls and

traps of the financial services industry and Harold's proven practical solutions to his own financial problems, we can help you take control of your financial life.

So by following the nine simple rules as outlined on our index card, you will

- have the confidence to make your own financial decisions;

- discover basic financial truths such as that low-fee index funds outperform just about any more complicated investment you can buy and that simple fixed-rate mortgages remain the best way to borrow money to buy your house;

- be armed with a timeless set of guidelines that you can turn to no matter what financial issues you may face or how drastically the winds of financial change shift; and

- be sure you never make the same mistake Sam made and let your fears about the financial unknown prevent you from doing anything.

Ready to finally take action and begin the next phase of your financial life?

Good. Let's get started.

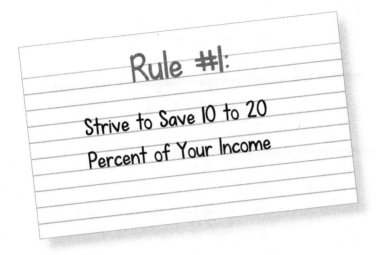

Rule #1:

Strive to Save 10 to 20 Percent of Your Income

LIFE HAPPENS: WHY YOU NEED TO SAVE MONEY

There comes a time when outside circumstances—what most people refer to as life—force us to take control.

For Harold, this moment came with the sudden arrival of his brother-in-law Vincent, which sent the household into fiscal chaos.

For most of us, however, it's not that sudden. Money comes in, and money goes out. It seems to simply vanish, lost in a windstorm of expected and unexpected expenses.

There's rent or mortgage, car payments, and the grocery bill. And honestly, who can even make sense of the average cell phone bill?

And those are just the monthly bills and regular expenses.

Then there are what might be termed the unexpected expected expenses. Take car repairs. Do you know anyone who ever planned for a broken-down car? On the other hand, do you know anyone who has ever had a car that didn't break down?

We want to be on top of our money, but instead we find ourselves avoiding thinking about it. It's natural, in a way. It can be difficult and the opposite of fun. But our avoidance prevents us from doing the most commonsense, basic thing we can do to take control of our financial life: *Learn how to save.*

WHY IT'S SO HARD TO SAVE–PART 1

Why do so many of us seem to come up short when playing the financial long game?

Well, take a breath. We're here to tell you that—wait for it . . .

It's not totally your fault.

If you find yourself working long hours, not spending extravagantly, and still wondering why you're not saving a dime, you're not alone. There are lots of things out there that make it hard for all of us to save.

In her book *Pound Foolish,* Helaine told the story of how many of our financial lives collapsed. The most important takeaway: For all too many of us, wages began to stagnate and fall. Accounting for inflation, the annual median income of American households declined by about $3,000 between 1998 and 2013. At the same time, income inequality has increased. Almost all gains in household income and wealth in the past several years have gone to the top 1 percent of the population, even the top 0.1 percent.

But just because our salaries were all but frozen didn't mean our cost of living enjoyed a similar break. Not only did the cost of all those things you can't live without— think health care, housing, and education—go up, but they have generally gone up faster than our salary increases and the costs of less essential items.

And even as we faced all these hurdles, we don't exactly live in a society that encourages moderation. In America, most of us idealize living large. Luxury is marketed at us incessantly. It's easy to tell people—not to mention ourselves—to ignore the millions of social cues that encourage us to overspend. It's certainly good advice but hard for all too many of us to heed.

When Helaine's older son was born in 1999, you would have been hard-pressed to spend more than $400 for a stroller, and that would have been a bulky, less-than-practical European import. Yet by the time her younger son was born in 2003, the $1,000 Bugaboo was (for a surprising number of us) suddenly a must-have. A $400 stroller seemed like a bargain-basement item. It was a great feat of marketing.

Watch any play-off game. Halftime ads feature a parade of amazing cars. Reprising his look from *The Matrix,* Laurence Fishburne hawks the new Kia K900 (manufacturer's suggested retail price $59,500). He intones that viewers should "challenge the luxury you know." He wants them to think about "the way it makes you feel."

All this seems counterintuitive given our tough economic times. How could we become *more* addicted to luxury spending? Yet research says it's just what we should expect to happen. According to economists Marianne Bertrand and Adair Morse, authors of a paper called "Consumption Contagion," the more the wealthier people at the top of the income ladder spend on high-status luxury goods, the greater the pressure to keep up across the income spectrum. This "trickle-down consumption," as they call it, reduces the savings rates for all too many of us.

The result?

- Our national savings rate has been in the low single digits for twenty-five years.

- A little more than a quarter (27 percent) of American households have net worths of $5,000 or less.

- 47 percent of us report that we could not come up with $400 if we needed to without selling something, resorting to increased credit card debt, borrowing from a friend or relative, or taking out a payday loan.

That's the world we live in. It isn't easy to step out.

WHY IT'S SO HARD TO SAVE—PART 2

The harder it is to make it through to the next day financially—whatever the reason—the harder you will find it to make careful and disciplined decisions. That's not because you are a bad person who wastes money and, thus, lands in financial hot water time and time again. It has to do with how we human beings are hardwired, the way we react to scarcity.

Imagine that your car payment is due. Your daughter comes home from school with a notice that you forgot to send in $25 for an upcoming field trip. The same day, you discover your mom needs help paying for her latest blood pressure medication.

This comes a mere two months after you moved into a new home. It seemed like the right thing to do. It's in a better school district. But the rent is higher, and that's stretching you in ways you didn't expect.

In all the confusion and panic, you forget the credit card payment is also due in two days. Suddenly you can add a $100 interest payment, not to mention the charge for late payment, to your financial woes.

Reading this, you are likely screaming, "*No!*" Don't turn to that overdraft protection with the hefty fee! You don't need another credit card! Just say no!

Someone—like you, for instance—intensely worrying about finances, however, is unlikely to think in that moment about the consequences of borrowing money. And it's not because you are uniquely financially irresponsible. The fact is if you're always worrying about your immediate cash flow, how to make it to next week or the next pay period, you are very likely to make mistakes.

When we want to build up body muscle strength, we slowly up our exercise routine. Jog a mile every day, and soon you'll find yourself able to jog a mile and a half. You've built up endurance.

According to Sendhil Mullainathan and Eldar Shafir, the authors of *Scarcity: Why Having Too Little Means So Much,* constantly scrambling to address money problems doesn't strengthen our money muscles. Indeed it has the opposite result. The more little decisions you need to make, the less likely you will be able to get the big ones right. Our money muscle doesn't strengthen. It weakens from stress and overuse.

Mullainathan—who happens to be an academic coauthor of Harold's—and Shafir call our self-defeating behavior "tunneling." And financial tunneling happens to all too many of us. So, no surprise, we all too often turn to credit to get by, whether for emergencies or that dinner out with friends at the hot new restaurant. As the commercial goes,

"There are some things money can't buy. For everything else there's MasterCard."

So now you are thinking, "Tell me again, how is all this supposed to make me feel better?" How is anything short of bare-bones financial survival even possible?

The answer, and repeat once more with feeling, is **Learn. How. To. Save.**

Without learning how to save, you won't be able to invest or pay down debt effectively. This is true no matter what your financial position.

How much should we save? you ask. Well, the title of this chapter pretty much says it: Ten to 20 percent of your gross income, the amount listed on your paycheck before taxes and everything else are taken out.

If you're already saving more, then kudos and feel free to move on to the next chapter. But for most of us, our progress is best measured out one small step at a time.

Just think about this: If you can put aside 10 percent of each paycheck, you will have more than one month's salary set aside in your first year! As an added bonus, you'll experience a whole lot less financial stress and drama along the way.

CREATE A FLEXIBLE AND REALISTIC
SPENDING AND SAVINGS PLAN

You can't begin to save until you educate yourself about where and how you are spending your money. Chances are you don't know. According to a 2013 survey by the pollster Gallup, two-thirds of us do not keep even the most rudimentary of budgets. That was certainly Harold's reality.

You need to determine what day-to-day spending is necessary and unavoidable, what is a luxury but helps you get through the day, and, finally, what is excess. Only then can you avoid falling prey to spending traps.

This allows you to make trade-offs: I'll take advantage of the office coffee machine, but I'll use the money I saved to travel to Italy next summer to attend my best friend's wedding. I'll drop my landline phone to pay for my gym membership or boost my child's college savings.

So how do you do this?

You can't do this by simply looking at your monthly bills. You need to look at everything. That's your day-to-day spending as well as your regular expenses.

Step 1: Monitor Your Spending

For three months, keep track of everything you spend money on, no matter how small. That $1.50 bag of Cape Cod Waffle Cut Sea Salt potato chips? It counts, just as much as your four-figure mortgage or health insurance payment.

It sounds like a time-consuming project, but it's not. websites, programs, or apps like Mint.com and Quicken .com will automatically collect and categorize every credit or debit card transaction. You can even snap pictures of your receipts with your smartphone. All you need to do at the beginning is sign on every couple of days to make sure they are assigning things to the proper categories, not to mention input cash spending. (If you wait more than a week, you will begin to forget what's what.)

You can't know what you are spending until you actually see the dollars and cents laid out right in front of you. Dividing every expense into categories like "Children's school expenses" and "Groceries" allows you to see the big picture. Otherwise, you don't know where your money is going.

Step 2: Confront Your Spending

At the end of the first month, look over your categories, and see how much you are spending in each. The first month will give you a sense of your recurring, nonnegotiable, non-discretionary expenses: rent or mortgage, health insurance, car payments, gas, child care, and so on.

Step 3: Refine Your Expenses over Time

If you monitor only one month of spending, you won't gain a full picture of where your money goes. Routine but sporadic expenses such as car repairs, doctor bills, and the emergency trip to the cat's vet are more likely to occur over a several-month period.

Over the period of three months, you'll get a good sense of your other expenses: pet care, entertainment, dining out, and the other things conveniently charged on your credit card at random intervals.

Step 4: Create a Plan

A realistic spending and savings plan accounts for how much you earn and how much you wish to spend, and it leaves room for flexibility: Money for dining out, say, can be repurposed if you spend a bit more on computer equipment one month than you had otherwise accounted for.

While many people call this budgeting, it's more helpful to think of it as surfing a financial wave. A budget sounds fixed. But while certain expenses can be planned and occur as regularly as waves—think of your rent or mortgage, for example—others cannot. As a result, the size and shape of this financial wave changes somewhat from month to month. One way to handle this? Know your regular and large expenses, monitor your other spending, and adjust as needed.

Step 5: Make Sure to Leave Room for Fun

See a movie, attend a concert, eat dinner out with a loved one a few times a month. Remember, starvation budgets work no better than starvation diets.

YOUR FIRST PRIORITY: SET MONEY ASIDE FOR AN EMERGENCY!

Think of saving as building a house. No matter how grandiose the house design, it won't stay up for long without a firm foundation, one without cracks that can withstand the elements.

Your budget's equivalent of a foundation is an emergency savings fund. This is the money you put aside for when things go wrong, and things go wrong for all of us.

An emergency fund brings stability and calm to your financial life. Instead of panicking at every little unexpected expense or needing to take money away from other wants and needs, you'll have a small pot of money at hand, ready for use.

What constitutes an emergency? An emergency is an expense that is both immediate and absolutely necessary. It almost certainly implies something bad has happened. An emergency is . . .

- root canal

- when the car breaks down on the side of the road

- any important or urgent medical matter

- when the heater blows in your home—and it's 22 degrees Fahrenheit outside

- losing your job—and with it your regular paycheck

To build your emergency fund, start stashing away three months of living expenses in an accessible savings account.

When we say three months of expenses, we don't mean three months of your take-home pay. We mean three months of your nonnegotiable living expenses, things like mortgage payments and grocery bills. This will give you breathing room if you suddenly lose a job while also offering a source of cash for the unexpected doctor bill.

DON'T SWEAT THE SMALL STUFF

As you begin to prioritize savings, you will almost certainly discover budgeting's cruel calculus. Unless you are a crazed shopaholic with the discipline of a dog eyeing a rare sirloin, count on your nondiscretionary expenses such as housing, transportation, and health care as being your largest outlays. They are also the ones offering the least flexibility—at least in the short run.

The experts say we should not spend more than 50 to 60 percent of our take-home pay on such expenses. Yet even if you realize you are spending $200 a month too much on rent and decide to find a cheaper place to live, you'll need to find the money to move—and even a short move to a nearby neighborhood can wipe out more than a year of savings.

Helaine likes to call this the non-latte factor. You've all heard of the Latte Factor. That's the term trademarked by the financial guru David Bach, who says if we just give up a $5 small luxury a day, we can retire millionaires. But if that were all it took, most of us would be millionaires already.

Helaine discovered the non-latte factor when she decided to cut a newspaper subscription bill, saving $40 a month. She was feeling great—until her health insurance company notified her that her premium would be raised by $100 a month the following year. The problem wasn't the paper she enjoyed reading. Her financial issue was the much larger expense she had little control over.

Your biggest outlays—like your house, like your car—are your biggest problems. It's important to get these right in the long run, but these expenses are harder to control in the immediate future. So what to do? There are no miracle cures here, no magic tips to make it all better. But there are commonsense stratagems you can use to get control of small expenses without feeling as if you were making huge sacrifices and give yourself some financial breathing room to deal with the big ones.

- Take all monthly bills and give them a good inspection. It's unlikely you can eliminate your cell phone bill, but does it really need to be that high? You'll likely notice fees and charges you don't understand. Ask someone to explain them to you. It's almost certain that either you are paying for things you don't need or you can negotiate for a lower monthly charge. Do you really need to rent that cable modem? (No.) Can't you live with a higher deductible on your home or auto insurance? (Almost certainly.)

- Scrutinize every line item on that monthly credit card bill. Harold found one exercise to be very useful. Imagine that someone stole your credit card and you had to cancel it. When your new card arrives, would you re-up for every magazine, iPhone app, or whatever else you're automatically paying for right now? When Harold performed this exercise, he discovered many accumulated items. Some had festered for years, including the $10 monthly charge for a wireless hot-spot service he never used, its password long forgotten. An annoying ninety minutes on hold later, and he was free.

- Make the time to better plan meals. Something worth remembering: According to the market research firm Natural Resources Defense Council, the average American family of four throws out between $1,365 and $2,275 worth of food annually. (Helaine would like it noted she wrote this sentence on a day when she tossed six strips of uncooked bacon found in a sandwich bag and an open but barely eaten package of lox in the trash because she had no idea how long either had been in the fridge.)

CASH IS KING

One way to cut back on spending is mind-numbingly simple but very hard to do in our society. Say good-bye to plastic and all virtual money. Studies have repeatedly demonstrated we will spend more—upward of 20 percent more—when we don't have to handle physical, paper dollar bills.

That includes debit cards. According to a group of researchers led by Manoj Thomas, a professor of marketing at Cornell University, consumers will impulsively purchase more junk food at the supermarket when they use a credit or debit card over cash. No doubt the same is true when we wave a smartphone app like Apple Pay or rely on credit or debit cards we've saved and stored on websites. Why? Paper and metal money are real. They are not abstract. It's painful to part with dollar bills one by one. Not so for the forms of money that don't seem like money. It doesn't feel like real money to us—until, that is, the bill comes due at the end of the month. Then it feels all too real.

When Helaine first began to write about personal finance, one standard tip given to people who thought they were overspending was to tell them to put their credit card in a glass of water and then place it in the freezer. If you wanted to buy something with it, you needed to defrost the water. The delay, conventional wisdom said, stopped a lot of casual spending. It's likely that's true. Listen to the entrepreneur Terri Trespicio, who went all cash for several weeks and then wrote about it:

> *I remember standing over a $3.89 container of dried cranberries, debating whether I'd get more satisfaction from gnawing on the fruit or from having that $4 in my pocket. (Ultimately, I chose the cash.) I made dinner at home instead of picking up takeout. When I did go out, I often decided to forego [sic] a second glass of wine and skipped entrees in favor of*

*bar snacks or appetizers—decisions that were proba-
bly as good for my waistline as my wallet.*

STARTS WITH AN *A:* SET UP AN AUTOMATIC SAVINGS PLAN

So how do you pry that money out of your wallet and get it
to start working for you, not against you?

Make it automatic.

When savings is automatic, the money goes into some
sort of separate account without your having to make it
happen every month and without its passing through your
own fingers with all the accompanying temptations.

For now, we don't need to think about *where* to invest
the money. We'll show in later chapters that this question
is easier than you might think. We also don't need to think
about whether we can afford to save, because . . . well, there
is always something.

If you work at a traditional job, when you sign up for
direct deposit, there is often an option for targeting some
of those funds for savings. Use it. If you are freelance like
Helaine, money comes in more erratically, and it is hard to
set a monthly target. So what does Helaine do? All incoming

funds are deposited to her savings account. She then grants herself a monthly "salary."

A motivational tip: Many banks, credit unions, and brokerages allow their customers to set up what we call sub-accounts. Those are accounts that operate under the rubric of your main account but sometimes (not always) have a different account number. This is a good one for people putting money aside for multiple goals, whether emergencies or winter getaways to the Caribbean. If you need some added incentive, consider giving your accounts names so the money doesn't feel so abstract. A few years ago, ING Direct (now Capital One) told the *New York Times* that the most common nicknames for their sub-savings accounts were the following:

1. Savings
2. Vacation
3. Emergency fund/rainy day
4. House
5. Taxes

DON'T PRIORITIZE EMERGENCY SAVINGS OVER CREDIT CARD DEBT

Meet Harold's friend Betty. She recently confided in Harold that she and her husband keep several thousand dollars in a checking account, even as they maintain several thousand dollars in credit card debt. "I like having that money there in case my furnace bursts."

Betty's not alone. Many other people do similar mental accounting. We all know where Betty's coming from. Having $4,000 cash money in the bank and owing $4,000 to Visa make many of us feel much more financially secure than having less money in the bank—and owing less money to Visa.

From a mathematical perspective, this makes no sense. Betty has spent thousands of dollars on unnecessary interest payments and related charges. Her furnace has never burst. Had she paid off that credit card bill, it's likely she would now have the money available to fix that furnace if it did need repair. Why? Because the thousands of dollars she's paid in interest payments could be resting comfortably in an emergency savings account. We're not suggesting you completely forgo an emergency savings account in favor of paying down debt. We just want you to maintain a healthy balance between the two if you find yourself in this position.

BEGIN THE FINANCIAL LIFTING WITH
ONE-POUND WEIGHTS

It's quite possible that if you weren't saving the proverbial blessed penny when you began this book, you will not be able to suddenly go from saving zero to saving 10 to 20 percent. Maybe you don't have the money to do that, at least right now. Maybe your debt payments are too large. Maybe you simply lack the practice.

Or maybe you do it for a few weeks and boom! You can't resist a new case for the iPhone. Don't beat yourself up. Sudden deprivation—which is what committed saving can feel like—rarely works. No one is perfect trying to lose weight. No one is perfect on a financial budget either. The important thing is to keep at it and to make steady progress without going crazy.

Saving 10 to 20 percent is the ultimate goal, not something you need to achieve yesterday afternoon. We don't want you to begin saving huge amounts of money, for instance, if you have any debts besides student loans and a mortgage. (Again, read the next chapter.) We want you to actually start today, do something, and keep it up so that you're following a realistic plan. It's better to save 1 percent consistently than try and fail over and over again to save 10 to 20 percent.

If you think you can't save, or if your attempts don't seem to be working, start small. Attempt to save 1 percent of your take-home pay. After a month, up this to 2 percent. After another month, make it 3 percent. And so on. By the end of the year, you should be saving close to 10 percent. The savings habit—unlike spending in a panic—is like a muscle. The more you use it, the stronger it will be. Think about it this way: No one expects you to start with a fifty-pound weight when you first go to the gym. That's why the one-pound weight exists.

Rule #2:

Pay Your Credit Card Balance in Full Every Month (and How to Deal with Other Forms of Debt)

GRANDMA'S BUDGETING SECRET: LACK OF EASY CREDIT

Almost no one goes into credit card debt deliberately. Just ask Harold.

Harold and Veronica spent most of their twenties and thirties owing money to Visa and MasterCard.

There was the rent bill and the day-care bill and seemingly constant and sometimes staggering repair bills for their clunky Dodge Caravan. There were the trips to visit family members back on the East Coast, many of which came with high price tags. There were the back-and-forth expenses for Veronica, who cared for her father during his final bout of lung cancer. There were the probably too frequent meals at Bob Evans, partly because everyone was too exhausted to cook every night. They had no emergency savings. How could they? They were using the high-interest plastic in their wallets as their go-to rainy day fund. It was a pretty tense time. They quarreled about money, about how to manage their monthly cash flow.

And Harold and Veronica were pretty lucky. Harold had a steady job, earning a respectable middle-class salary. They contributed to a retirement account. They kept up with their minimum credit card payments. They weren't among the third of households every year with an unpaid bill turned over to a collection agency. They weren't bouncing checks, juggling payments, trying to decide which payment could be safely ignored while tossing a few extra dollars at a more persistent creditor. Occasionally, Harold would pick up an extra gig and pay off the entire balance, only to soon repeat the cycle.

Many of us spend a lot of our lives in debt. Average

credit card debt per U.S. household now exceeds $7,000. But it's actually worse than that. A little more than half of us manage to pay off our credit card bill in full every month. The rest of us? Take the financial Boy Scouts out of the picture, and the remaining households owe an average of more than $15,000.

We beat ourselves up constantly for getting into debt messes. We're convinced our grandparents possessed some special financial discipline that we lack.

Not true.

It's almost certain the secret to our grandparents' extraordinary financial discipline was a result of the four *L*s:

- lack of access to credit
- layaway plans
- loved ones
- loan sharks

Lack of Access to Credit

Once upon a time, as Elizabeth Warren and Amelia Warren Tyagi pointed out in their personal finance guide *All*

Your Worth, easy credit did not exist. No one needed to exercise much in the way of financial discipline when going into a store. You literally couldn't fall prey to temptation about that pretty dress or camera lens you didn't have the money to buy *right at that moment.* Instead, stores offered layaway plans, allowing customers to pay a small amount toward a purchase week after week until it was completed. Only then could you take it home.

Sometimes the local butcher offered credit to regular customers. But he needed to know you and know you were good for the money on payday. And while in an emergency you could turn to loved ones for help with the rent money, they were unlikely to be sympathetic to a plea for that must-have newfangled television thing. They would tell you to save up for it or put it on layaway. And most people sensibly avoided loan sharks. Remember that scene in *The Sopranos* when Tony is driving with Christopher, and he spots a guy who owes him a few? Actually, Harold doesn't remember this, because he's too cheap to get HBO. But you get the point. Fists were involved.

Things change. Today, the average American who has a credit card has 3.7 of them. You can hardly go shopping without being offered 10 percent off on all your purchases that day if you apply for a store-branded card *right this minute*. Hospitals and doctors and dentists—not to mention veterinarians—now offer access to fast credit via CareCredit.

And we haven't even gotten to subprime auto loans, payday loans, pawnshops, rent-to-own, refund loans, loans disguised as convenient payment plans, and other adventures in high-interest lending that capitalize on consumers' impatience, innumeracy, or simple despair.

How did this happen? Over time, credit loosened up. Usury laws—that is, laws that limited personal credit interest rates—were greatly relaxed beginning in the 1970s. Modern credit scoring allowed credit card issuers to gauge how likely different people were to promptly, or eventually, pay these loans.

This data crunching advanced to the point where financial services companies determined that the best way for them to operate was to not lend money to the most well-heeled borrowers. Come again? you may ask.

Well, the real money for credit card issuers is in *making sure people who can't or don't pay off their bills in full load up on credit, then charging them for the privilege*. As a result, they don't want you to manage your money responsibly. If you do, they'll call you a deadbeat. Why? They don't make any money off you. If you use your card to buy something like an appliance, then pay off your bill at the end of the month, you are costing them money because they can't charge you any fees.

But use the credit card as an expensive loan, and you are a profit center. But unlike the loan sharks of old, purveyors of these forms of credit can't break your thumbs if you don't fully pay. Your creditors will pummel you emotionally instead, hoping to drain a few extra dollars out of you.

BE A "DEADBEAT": PAY OFF YOUR BILLS EVERY MONTH

It feels as if we can never escape.

But we can. We just need to try to surmount the temptation, not to mention the need, to use high-interest credit to get by. High-interest debt can grow so fast it will overwhelm your other savings and investments.

There is no better way to simplify and gain control over your financial life than by eliminating high-interest debt.

So pay off your credit card and other high-interest loans ASAP. For most of us, this is by far the best investment opportunity we'll ever receive.

Think of it this way: The average interest rate on credit

card balances is around 15 percent. On store-branded cards, it is higher, often between 20 and 25 percent. That's the rate of return you receive, tax-free and risk-free, when you pay that debt down. No other investment reliably earns anything close to that. So there's nothing more important in your financial life than to pay that down.

PAY MORE THAN THE MINIMUM

When you receive a statement from a credit card company, it will come with a minimum payment requirement.

That minimum payment amount listed on your statement is not a recommendation. Unfortunately, all too many of us take this minimum payment as just that. According to economists Jialan Wang and Benjamin Keys, a third of us will pay the minimum almost every month, with another third sometimes paying the bill in full but also often paying, yes, the minimum. Only one-third of us use credit cards fully in lieu of carrying cash or checks and pay them off regularly at the end of every billing cycle.

Why are so many of us paying only the minimum? Many of us probably can't afford to pay more. But others are likely falling prey to a concept cognitive psychologists call anchoring. We see the prominently displayed minimum payment, and we believe it's the right thing to do. The credit card company is saying it's okay. It wouldn't mislead us, would it? So we make that payment, or something near to it, and feel okay. We shouldn't. Paying the minimum when you can afford to pay more takes a lot of money out of your pocket and gives it away to the credit card company. When credit card companies say it could take you more than five years to pay off that restaurant splurge, they aren't kidding.

RANK YOUR DEBT

Can't pay all your bills off right away?

Then you need to begin by ranking your debt.

Sit down with all of your bills. That's right, all of them. Not just credit cards. But car loans and student loans too. You need to work out the following:

1. What you owe each lender
2. What the interest rate and other expenses are for each loan

It shouldn't be that hard, practically speaking, because if you have followed our advice from the last chapter, you'll have everything online, contained within your spending and savings plan.

Emotionally, it might be a difficult experience. You'll likely feel anger, regret, and sadness. It might feel as if every financial, work, or personal mistake were right in front of you. It's quite possible you'll recall the vacation taken with an ex-boyfriend or ex-girlfriend to save a relationship that couldn't be saved or the bills you ran up when you were suddenly downsized with two weeks' severance. Maybe you should have bought a less expensive car or not fallen for the short-term zero-interest loan offered by a local furniture store. Perhaps you'll wonder if you could have gotten through college with fewer student loans. It's okay to acknowledge the mistakes and the roads not taken. But then it is time to take action.

PAY DOWN THE BILL WITH THE HIGHEST INTEREST RATE FIRST

The interest rate you are charged on your credit card is called the annual percentage rate, often shortened to APR. At the beginning of 2015, the annual median rate offered is in the midteens, with those deemed a higher credit risk paying upward of 20 percent.

You have at least twenty-one days from the day the bill is mailed to pay your bill without incurring interest charges. Pay your credit card in full—like one-third of all customers—and you are indeed receiving an interest-free loan. If you don't, the interest immediately begins to accrue. And once you miss a full payment, you'll pay a high interest rate on your balance all the time, until the next time you pay your entire bill.

Skip a payment, pay below the minimum amount, pay late, or exceed your monthly credit limit, and get ready for the pain in the form of various immediate penalties. And you are subsequently charged a penalty interest rate, which is typically much higher. How long will you have to pay this higher rate? The language on Harold's credit card agreement says obliquely that this rate "may apply indefinitely."

So paying down or—better—paying off your credit card debt is the best financial investment you'll ever get to make.

But all debt is not created equal. Every form of debt has its own interest rate. How does that work? Well, let's say you owe $5,000 on one credit card with a 25 percent interest rate and $2,500 on another card that carries a 10 percent interest rate. (We've dramatically simplified this example to illustrate a general point.) Let's also assume you have to make a minimum payment of $25 per month on each card and that you have $150 available right now to pay down the two debts.

There are, of course, several ways to divide up this $150. You can pay $75 to each card. You can make the minimum payment on the big debt while you concentrate on paying off the smaller debt. Or you can choose the opposite strategy of paying down the higher-interest-rate card first, making the minimum payment on the other. (You could of course skip payments or pay less than the minimum. Just don't do that.)

At the end of three years, these strategies yield very dif-

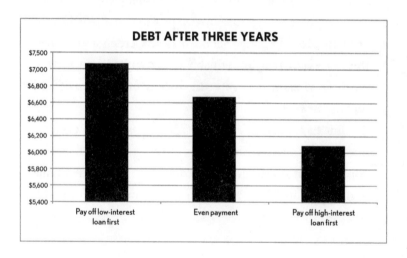

ferent results. Without paying a penny more, you save almost $1,000 by prioritizing your most costly debt.

This is why interest rates matter. The fastest way of ending your debt drama and getting off the debt treadmill is to devote your resources to paying down the bill with the highest interest rate while paying the required minimum on the rest. When you've retired that bill, you move on to the debt with the next-highest interest rate.

Some argue for a different strategy: Make a list of all the debts, and pay them down in order from the smallest to the largest. You can think of this as the momentum method. Does this approach work better? For some people, maybe. A study published in 2012 by two professors at Northwestern University's Kellogg School of Management found that the more bills people were able to put to bed—no matter what the amount—the more likely they were to work their way out of debt.

You have to know yourself. If you need the psychic boost that comes with putting to bed your small debts, consider that approach. But know it will cost you. And the higher the interest rates on your loans, the more you will pay over time.

DON'T GO IT ALONE: FIND AN ACCOUNTABILITY PAL

So how can you surmount your initial urge to pay off the smallest amounts over the highest interest rates? How do you slowly chip away at your mountain of debt, a process that can sometimes take years of hard work and financial trade-offs? How do you stop using your credit card to purchase everything from pick-me-ups to groceries?

Get an accountability pal. That's a friend or relative you can check in with every so often, to make sure you are on track. Don't underestimate how much outside cheerleading can help. Take Ellie, Meredith, and Joan. The three women met when they signed up for a six-week personal finance class offered by their city's college alumni organization. Over the course of the sessions, they became friendly and realized they were all there to knock out debt and get a grip on their savings. So after the class ended, they made a pact to meet once a month, talk over their progress, share their successful (and occasionally unsuccessful) strategies. Ultimately, another three women from the class joined them. After two years, the group of now six women had collectively knocked out tens of thousands of dollars in debt. And that wasn't all. Meredith, who dreamed of going out on her own, left her job and opened her own graphic design business. "We needed the strength of the group," Ellie said. "When I started, I had no savings and carried a huge amount of debt. It's just what everyone I knew did, so I did it too."

If you don't want to turn to your personal circle, there are also online groups that can perform this function, such as Frugal Village. Support gives an added boost, bucking you up when you feel as if you can't do it and making you feel less alone in your battle.

IT NEVER HURTS TO ASK: TRY TO NEGOTIATE YOUR CREDIT CARD BILL

One way to pay off your bills faster is to negotiate lower interest rates. After all, the lower the rate, the slower the bill will grow. How do you do this? Call each and every one of your creditors, and see if you can lower the interest rate on the debt you currently owe.

Will it work? It depends. The credit card companies don't want to see you transfer your balance to a lower-interest credit card offer or, even worse in their view, turn to the bankruptcy courts. Don't be shy, and don't be embarrassed about your financial position. The worse that can happen is that your credit card company says no. But we can guarantee you won't get anywhere if you don't try at all.

Another common strategy is to move the debt from one credit card to another, chasing introductory interest transfer offers, not to mention a permanent lower interest rate. This is called a balance transfer. It's not a bad strategy—provided, that is, you don't rack up more debt on your new credit card. Why? Many of these deals come with a significant gotcha—that all the new debt will be issued at a higher interest rate than the one offered for your balance transfer.

Another catch to watch out for: Don't mindlessly follow the advice of online credit card comparison websites for the best low-interest or balance-transfer deal out there. According to the *Wall Street Journal,* many either highlight the cards of their advertisers over better offers or bow to pressure from banks and credit card companies to show their fees and interest rates in the best possible light.

REDUCE YOUR CREDIT CARD SPENDING–AND GIVE YOURSELF A REWARD

If you are tempted to over-rely on your credit card or borrow more money, you are going to make it even harder to pay off your revolving balances. When you commit to paying down your credit card bills, you should avoid running up more debt on them. If at all possible, use cash, a debit card, or a prepaid card to make purchases.

Finally, don't fall for credit card rewards programs. Of course it's nice to have a free airline ticket or statement credit. It's so nice that the lure of these rewards likely leads you to be less vigilant about spending. A study of one such program showed that consumers received an average monthly cash-back reward of $25. People's monthly spending on these cards increased by $76, and their debt on these cards increased by $197. That's a bad deal.

Our suggestion: Reduce your own credit card spending, and then buy yourself a prize.

BEWARE OF DEBT CONSOLIDATORS

Proceed with caution if you are thinking about debt consolidation or debt counseling. Debt consolidation is when an organization such as a bank, credit union, or company specializing in debt management pays off all your debts. In return, you pay the organization back. That means one monthly bill, not a dozen or dozens. It might well be for a smaller amount than you were paying multiple creditors on your own.

Well, first, it's not free. Debt consolidation is still debt. It might be at a lower interest rate than the other debt but maybe not. If the monthly bill seems lower than what you were paying on your own, it might be because of lower interest rates, or it might be because you lengthened the payment period, actually increasing your total tab.

But all that pales in the face of another downside: Debt consolidation loans need to be secured by a possession; that's usually a car or a home. Fall behind on this loan, and you are putting your car or your house at risk of repossession.

Then there is debt settlement. Consumers confuse it with consolidation. They shouldn't. Debt settlement is when you turn to a debt counselor, who will attempt to negotiate partial forgiveness for the debt on your behalf.

Unfortunately, more than a few debt settlement counselors and consolidators are poor business citizens. Many jack up the fees, leaving the desperate consumers who turned to them in worse shape than when they began the process. Others don't even contact creditors on your behalf at all. It can be very hard for the typical consumer to tell the difference between the good guys and the goons. The standard advice for dealing with debt counselors is to tell consumers to use a nonprofit service such as the National Foundation for Credit Counseling. However, it's important to remember even the most honest players can have conflicts of interest. Some of the nonprofits funded with bank and credit card money, for instance, will rarely recommend bankruptcy, no matter how dire your situation.

Many people are now turning to peer-to-peer lending sites as a sort of do-it-yourself debt consolidation. Companies like the Lending Club use sophisticated algorithms to determine who is most likely to pay the money back versus who is in danger of defaulting. It's a great deal—if you can get it. Unfortunately, many are not able to utilize this method. The people who need help the least are the most likely to get it, thanks to those algorithms.

All in all, if you are so desperate you are turning to debt consolidators and debt counselors to get out from under, you might be better off chatting with a bankruptcy attorney instead.

On that note . . .

DO NOT BE ASHAMED TO DECLARE BANKRUPTCY

There were about 900,000 personal bankruptcy filings in the United States in 2014. While there is this pervasive myth out there that all too many of us fecklessly charge up consumer goods and then turn to the courts to get out from under when the debt blows up in our faces, the truth is much more depressing. Most of us end up in financial trouble because of the economic plagues of the twenty-first century—health-care bills, unemployment, and family collapse. Moreover, the evidence suggests that most of us wait too long to declare bankruptcy, draining retirement accounts that would otherwise be safe from creditors once we seek the protections of the courts, in an increasingly hopeless effort to keep up with our bills.

So repeat after us:

> *There is no shame in admitting we can't keep up.*
> *There is no shame in declaring bankruptcy.*

Now take a deep breath. Bankruptcy is not an easy process, but it just might be easier than dedicating years of your life to paying off bills that the courts would agree are too much for you to handle on your income and assets.

There are two types of bankruptcy. If you have lots of debts and little in the way of assets, you can file for Chapter 7. After a review of the situation, your debts will be wiped out, and you can start your financial life anew. If, however, you own a home or other assets you would like to protect from creditors, you file for Chapter 13. You'll work out a three- to five-year repayment plan that won't leave you destitute. At the end of that period, any debts you still cannot pay off will be discharged.

Are there downsides? Of course. Access to credit is likely to be difficult for several years. Some future employers are likely to look down on it, but then again, those same employers may not hire you because of a low credit score, which you will almost certainly have if you can't keep up with your bills. On the other hand, you can no longer be hassled by debt collectors or others seeking to collect the money you owe them. The law prohibits them from contacting you once you file for bankruptcy.

Moreover, several types of debt are not eligible to be discharged in bankruptcy. These include IRS liens and child support payments. As for student loan debt, you need to prove "undue hardship"—a very tough standard to meet.

However, declaring bankruptcy might well give you

peace of mind. Many people who have been through the process say their only regret is that they wish shame had not kept them from turning to the courts for relief sooner. There are no points to be gained from attempting to pay bills you cannot keep up with. After all, no one wakes up in the morning and thinks, "What a great day to go into debt."

HANDLE STUDENT LOANS LIKE A PRO

The Federal Reserve estimates Americans owe $1.3 trillion in student debt. While people under forty are responsible for two-thirds of that debt, the amount owed by older people, even senior citizens, is soaring too. Studies have shown student loan debt affects everything from home ownership to marriage, even retirement. These loans that we assume to help train us for adulthood often end up determining it instead.

What's more, many people sign up for student loans without paying attention to the actual loan, let alone the fine print. A recent study published by the Brookings Institution found half of college freshmen thought they had borrowed less money than they had. Among all first-year students with federal loans, 28 percent reported having no federal debt and 14 percent said they didn't have any student debt at all.

Unfortunately, thanks to the fact that the cost of higher education has increased at a rate significantly more than the rate of inflation—not to mention our salaries—since the 1980s, many of us are not in a position to avoid taking out loans to pay for college. But there are things you can do to make the situation a bit easier.

First, know what kinds of loans you have. We can borrow money to attend college from either the federal government or private banks. It's quite possible you have both types of loans.

You should always borrow from the federal government first. Why? Federal loans offer much more flexibility than privately issued loans. There are different monthly payment plans based on income. In some cases you can defer payment if you return to school or are underwater financially. More generous options are available if you work in selected public service occupations too. The Department of Education provides an informative website, StudentAid .ed.gov, that runs through the options and fine print on student loans and where to go for help. Visit it.

The issuers of private student loans are much less forgiving and flexible than the federal government. Unlike with federal loans, the interest rate does not need to be fixed. That leaves your financial life more than a bit uncertain. And if your income isn't high enough to meet your private monthly student loan payments? Well, too bad. Sometimes the bank will help, and sometimes it won't, and you won't have much in the way of recourse.

As a result, this is a rare case where even if the amount owed on the federal loan is at a higher interest rate than your other bills, we'd strongly suggest you pay down almost every other bill you have before you take this one on.

Quick note about consolidating student loans: This can be very tempting. For starters, it allows you to pay one or two bills a month instead of making payments to what could be several different lenders. It also reduces the overall monthly payment, freeing up cash for other uses.

No-brainer, right?

Not quite. As with other consolidated loans, the lower monthly payment might well come at the cost of lengthening the term of the loan and increasing the amount of money you are going to pay over time. What's more, consolidating federal student loans is, in the vast majority of cases, a onetime offer. There are no do-overs, unless you return to school and acquire more federal student debt. The best place to begin the process of figuring out if consolidation is right for you is to check out the Department of Education's website.

At no point should you turn to private counselors or services offering to help you reduce the load of your student debt repayments. According to a report issued by the National Consumer Law Center, these are almost always high-priced and fee-ridden consolidation services interested in padding their own bottom lines and less concerned about protecting yours.

One other potential pitfall: Do not combine federal and private student loans. Why? Once again, federal loans provide more flexibility in the event of financial hardship, and you will lose those benefits if you consolidate those loans with a private lender.

Finally, if you can't keep up, don't be an ostrich! Don't go into default; that is, don't simply stop paying your monthly bill. The penalty fees will pile up fast. Instead, look for help. A good place to start is the website of the Consumer Financial Protection Bureau, ConsumerFinance.gov, or the Department of Education. These sites offer unbiased guidance and tell you how to ask for help and what you need to do to receive it.

YOU'RE OUT OF DEBT, NOW WHAT?

Now that you are out of debt, remember to pay off your credit card bill in full every month if you can. If you can't do it, take it as a sign to immediately retire the card until the debt is gone.

Debt all too often happens to us when we are working to improve our lives but meanwhile need to just get through the day. Don't let it steal your future. It won't be easy to pay off or otherwise eliminate consumer debt from your life, but the results will be worth it. Just ask Harold. As we wrote this chapter, his wife and daughter went off to Paris on vacation. No debt required.

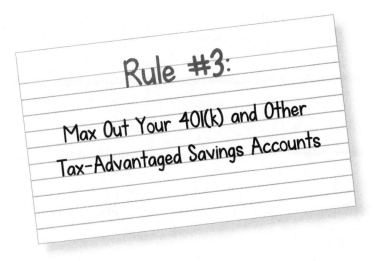

Rule #3:

Max Out Your 401(k) and Other
Tax-Advantaged Savings Accounts

AFTER EMERGENCY SAVINGS AND CREDIT CARDS, FOCUS ON RETIREMENT

It's your first day at the new job. There are papers to fill out and sign. There are health insurance decisions to be made and federal and state tax forms to complete. Then there is the form asking you how much of your salary you want to set aside for your retirement. It seems so far off, and you could use the money now. Plus there's all that tiny print, and it's pretty complicated. So you put it aside for later, and—

Stop right there.

After your emergency fund, saving for retirement is probably the most important savings you'll ever undertake. When it comes to planning for retirement, playground rules apply—no do-overs.

If you don't begin putting away money today, you will almost certainly regret it tomorrow. If you begin retirement savings in your twenties, you will be in a better position to maintain your standard of living after you stop receiving a paycheck. Wait until your forties . . . and it will be much harder. Some analysts say you'll need to save more than a third of your salary to catch up.

Harold didn't follow this advice very well. On his very first day at his very first job, the Dow Jones Industrial Average was level at about 1,500. That was a long time ago. As we sat down to write this chapter, the Dow sat at 18,024. By ignoring the boring forms (and then getting a late start professionally), Harold missed out on one of the biggest run-ups in stock market history. Only by beginning to put aside 20 percent of his pretax income at age forty was Harold finally able to start catching up. Still, he could have been on a much more comfortable path had he only been more diligent at that first workplace, almost thirty years ago.

THINK BIG

Once upon a time, there was no such thing as retirement. Most people didn't live long enough to voluntarily leave the workforce, which was often the family farm. Seniors depended upon their children and other relatives. The combination of industrialization and improved health care changed a centuries-old system. Many lived longer, but a depressing number of elderly people were abandoned when they could no longer work.

Over the course of the twentieth century, the introduction of Social Security and then Medicare, combined with the growth of corporate and public sector pensions and healthy private savings, made our senior years comfortable and manageable for so many of us.

Then things got tougher.

Outside the public sector, pensions—also known as defined benefit plans—for new hires are becoming as rare as four-leaf clovers, replaced by do-it-yourself plans like the 401(k). As for

Social Security, what's known as the replacement rate is falling. In the 1980s, we could expect our Social Security check to make up for about half of our preretirement salary. Someone retiring now can expect to receive only a 40 percent replacement rate. In another ten years, that will fall to 36 percent.

We're living longer than ever after we retire. On average, Americans who reach age sixty-five can now expect to reach age eighty-four. More than a quarter of sixty-five-year-olds can expect to reach age ninety. How far off are we from meeting our late-life financial needs? Suffice it to say that a large minority of baby boomers and a solid majority of Gen Xers are expected to be unable to maintain their standards of living in retirement.

Surveys routinely find about half of us are petrified of running out of money in retirement. Unfortunately, our first response is denial. Surveys also show most of us have not tried to figure out what we need for retirement or how to accomplish it.

They are like Jack. He's a successful corporate administrator in his early forties. He puts money aside for retirement. But how much? He's not sure. He does what his accountant tells him. And besides, he confesses, it's not as if that 401(k) were only for retirement. It's there for emergencies and his children's schooling too. Anyway, it's not that big of a deal, is it? He's healthy. "I'll work as long as I want," he claims. "My skills are in demand."

DON'T COUNT ON WORKING FOREVER

We've heard many people say things along the lines of what Jack says. "I'll work until I drop" is a popular one. "I'll never retire" is another. Sounds like a nice idea, right? And sometimes it really does work out that way. Helaine's grandma Ann, who worked for a religious day school, remained on the job until she was ninety-three. She loved her work and didn't want to leave. She was a working mom before the term ever existed.

Grandma Ann was so devoted to her work that when she finally left after breaking a bone in a fall at the school, she went out on worker's comp. She was that sure she'd be returning to her job.

All of which is to say that we don't always get to choose the when and why of retiring, not even a ninety-three-year-old worker bee like Grandma Ann.

But we refuse to believe it. Even though only about 20 percent of us remain employed past the age of sixty-five, most of us continue to think we will be the exception. In fact, a majority of retirees leave the workforce earlier than they had planned. Often, earlier-than-planned retirement is brought about by health difficulties or by family caregiving needs. The recent recession and downsizing have played significant roles too. So does age discrimination.

In other words, life happens. We want you to be prepared if it happens to you. And no, practicing saying, "Do you want fries with that?" is not a plan. It's an assumption you won't ever need a hip or knee replacement and will be able to take a job that demands you remain on your feet for hours at a time.

START YOUNG

I'm too young to think about putting money aside for my old age. I don't plan to retire for decades anyway.

Actually, this is the perfect time to begin saving. Why? Because of the basic logic of compound interest.

What do we mean by compounding? Well, when you put money aside early, you can reinvest your investment profits. And over the decades, these can really grow. Let's say you start at age twenty-five and you save $104 every month for forty years to finance your retirement. Now let's assume you've put that in an investment that provides a good-but-not-insane predictable 6 percent annual return. You'll have about $200,000 by age sixty-five.

If you want to accumulate that same $200,000 and you begin putting the money aside at the age of forty-five, you'll need to put aside about four times as much—$430 a month—just about the time you'll likely be paying for more and more life expenses like home repair bills and children leaving for college. Things get worse from there.

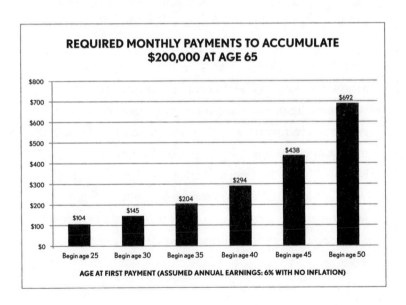

**REQUIRED MONTHLY PAYMENTS TO ACCUMULATE
$200,000 AT AGE 65**

Begin age 25	$104
Begin age 30	$145
Begin age 35	$204
Begin age 40	$294
Begin age 45	$438
Begin age 50	$692

AGE AT FIRST PAYMENT (ASSUMED ANNUAL EARNINGS: 6% WITH NO INFLATION)

Of course, this is grossly simplified. The stock market is unpredictable. It has done well historically, but no one can say exactly what your returns will be if you will need to withdraw the money earlier than you planned. But here is the one thing we know:

You will absolutely be better off putting money aside than if you don't.

An early start has other advantages too. It lets you ride out the stock market's periodic busts and booms. Harold really started to save for retirement in 2003, when he took his new job. He and the university have been steadily contributing ever since.

His timing wasn't great. The 2008 stock market crash actually wiped out Harold's lifetime investment profits to that point. That was a bummer, but he had thirty years to go. He was lucky enough to stay employed. He kept putting money aside in stock index funds. He has since greatly benefited from the stock market's subsequent recovery. Yes, it's likely there will be more bad years ahead. But there will probably be good years too. He believes that the power of compounding will continue to work to his benefit.

RETIREMENT ACCOUNTS = TAX-FAVORED SAVINGS

But can't I just use a brokerage account?

Yes, you can. But you shouldn't—at least until you max out your retirement and other tax-advantaged savings accounts. Why? Used correctly, officially sanctioned retirement accounts offer big tax benefits that can substantially increase your long-term investment gains. We pay taxes annually on the capital gains—ranging from stock sales to dividend payments—from regular brokerage accounts. Retirement accounts, on the other hand, are allowed to grow tax-free, and that allows more money to compound. There are often other tax benefits, too, which we mention below.

Simply put, *there is no better, more effective, or more lucrative way to begin building and growing your long-term savings than to make proper use of your defined contribution retirement account.*

TAKE ADVANTAGE OF YOUR WORKPLACE RETIREMENT PLAN

So let's try this again: It's your first day on the job.

What are you looking at?

The most common workplace retirement plan is called the 401(k); in the nonprofit world, it's called a 403(b), which is basically the same thing. These plans get their less-than-scintillating names from the pertinent sections of the federal tax code. Both the 401(k) and the 403(b) permit employees to put aside a percentage of their pretax salary and allow employers to contribute too. The money comes out of your salary directly and is sent to the retirement account without your ever seeing it in your day-to-day direct deposit bank account.

The money put aside in these accounts isn't taxed until you start to withdraw it. You are allowed to do so without penalty when you reach the age of fifty-nine and a half. You don't escape taxes entirely. Your withdrawals will be taxed as if they were earned income, like the money you receive in return for performing a job. But you'll take most of the money after retirement, when you will likely be in a lower tax bracket. So this is a good deal. (If you're not in a lower bracket in retirement, it's because you've become pretty rich. As Helaine's other grandma, Nana Sara, was fond of saying, "You should only have such problems.")

The initial paperwork can take . . . um . . . two forms.

Many companies that ask you to sign up for the 401(k) or other retirement plan, ask what percentage of your salary you would like to see taken out on a tax-deferred basis, and ask how you would like to invest the money.

Another group will hand you papers explaining that you've automatically opted into the company's retirement plan. That means a percentage of your salary is deferred into your company's retirement plan. No more, no less. If you want to change it, you need to fill out other papers.

As we said before, this is the point when most folks take all this paperwork and shove it in their desk drawer, where it then serves as cover for a secret stash of M&M's. Again, *do not make this mistake*—forget about your retirement, that is. We have nothing against M&M's.

Look at the opt-in papers and decide what percent you wish to defer. If you receive the opt-out papers, you also need to decide what percent you wish to defer because the amount your company is automatically deducting is almost certainly too low.

Let us explain: Companies need to set an opt-out rate that encourages employees to participate without scaring people off. So the amount automatically set aside is often about 3 percent. Unless you are expecting to win the Mega Millions jackpot or believe you will inherit the long-lost fortune of a forgotten relative, this isn't enough.

So what should you put aside? Most experts say you need to consider saving between 10 and 15 percent of your gross pay to ensure you have a decent living standard in retirement. If you have a comfortable income now relative to your current needs, your 401(k) is a good place to save—right up to the legal limit. This is the main way Harold caught up on his retirement savings.

NEVER, EVER FORGO THE EMPLOYER MATCH

"I can't afford to save that much, at least right now," we can hear you screaming. "I can barely get an emergency fund together, never mind save for some far-off event like getting old." We get it. Maybe you are trying to pay down debts. Maybe you want to save for a house. Maybe you are trying to boost your emergency fund. Maybe you are saving up for a once-in-a-lifetime trip.

If so, look at something called the employer match, which is when your employer agrees to match a certain portion of the salary you set aside in your retirement account. A majority of employers who offer their employees a 401(k) do this. They want to encourage their employees—that's you—to put money aside.

There is often an employer match on what you put aside, usually up to 3 to 6 percent of your annual earnings, depending on your employer's policy. If you don't put money aside, there is no match. It's as if someone said if you put $10 of your $100-a-week salary in a wallet and agree to not spend it, I'll pay you a larger salary. Helaine's children would never turn down such an offer. Neither should you. But many of us do. According to Financial Engines, one in four workers offered matches do not contribute enough money to take full advantage of the benefit, costing themselves an average of $1,336 annually.

No surprise, almost every personal finance advisor or guru suggests contributing to your retirement account up to the eligible match amount even when you are paying down credit card debt. Why? If your employer offers a retirement account with a match, this is likely the best shot you will ever get at earning money for doing absolutely nothing. Don't turn it down.

KNOW THE DIFFERENCE BETWEEN IRAS, ROTH IRAS, AND SEP-IRAS

What if I want to save more money than I can in my 401(k)? Or what if my company—like about 50 percent of employers—doesn't offer one at all?

Individual retirement accounts (IRAs) were set up in the 1970s to encourage people to save for retirement. In a way, they were the 401(k)s before there were real 401(k)s.

If you are not covered by a retirement plan where you work, you can put up to $5,500 into an IRA and another $1,000 if you are over fifty. The traditional IRA offers an immediate tax deduction, and the money grows tax-free, but withdrawals in retirement will be taxed as though they were earned income, like a 401(k).

You can still contribute to an IRA if you are covered by a workplace plan, but the fine print depends on your income. Google "IRA contribution limits" and "irs.gov" for details. If you have a comfortable six-figure income, consult an accountant who can get things right.

If you have a side gig or you operate your own business, you should open a Simplified Employee Pension IRA (SEP-IRA), which offers similar tax advantages. You can contribute 25 percent of your self-employment income to your SEP-IRA, up to a high limit that in 2015 totaled $53,000.

Then there is the Roth IRA. It doesn't offer an immediate deduction, and money is contributed on an after-tax basis. But as long as you obey some simple rules, which we'll discuss in a minute, your Roth contributions and their investment gains will never be taxed again.

Then there is the new myRA. Employees who work for firms that do not offer a retirement investing plan are eligible to contribute through direct deposit. The money is invested in guaranteed, low-expense, low-interest government funds. Your myRA balance is capped at $15,000. When you surpass that amount, the money will be moved to a financial services account.

What to do?

If you are financially stretched, consider taking an immediate deduction with the traditional IRA. You can use the savings to pay down credit card debt or pursue some other long-term goal. If you feel more financially secure, go for the Roth. But whatever you do, make your IRA or Roth IRA deposits automatic. By regularly contributing throughout the year, you spare yourself hassle at tax time. You'll also be less likely to fritter away money on nonessentials. As for a myRA, it's a nice way to get a savings habit started.

Whatever you do, know that you are better off contributing to any IRA than you would be not using one at all.

NEVER TAKE MONEY FROM A RETIREMENT ACCOUNT UNLESS YOU ARE OUT OF OPTIONS

The chances are quite good you will need or want some retirement money at some point before retirement. About one-third of us are currently "borrowing" money from our own 401(k)s, something retirement industry insiders call "leakage." We do it when we encounter medical emergencies, or have to pay our children's college expenses. Others withdraw money from workplace and personal retirement accounts when they change jobs whether they need the money or not. Most of that money will never be replaced.

The strength and weakness of the American retirement account system is that you can access your money at any time if you need it. That's great because it can give you a sense of security when things get tough. But that flexibility lets us undermine our long-term savings through mistakes, impatience, panic, and, yes, need.

Ask Harold. He's borrowed from his retirement savings on occasion. It was better than owing big credit card debt. That was the only good thing about it. Many friends have confessed that they view their retirement account money as emergency savings, slightly difficult to access but available if they need it. What do we think? We think it is best to leave this money alone. On the other hand, life, as we are fond of saying, happens. It might be better to withdraw the money than run up credit card debt if you are downsized and have no other financial alternatives.

The law is set up to discourage you from taking money out of a retirement account until you are at least fifty-nine and a half years old. It's not forbidden—frankly, you can do it with a few taps on your keyboard—but you will almost certainly be charged for the privilege. Not only will you pay taxes on many of the withdrawals, but the U.S. government imposes an additional 10 percent surcharge for the privilege of accessing your own money most of the time.

This isn't the result of mean-spirited lawmaking. It's meant to encourage you to leave your funds alone. However, our lawmakers realized that you might need the money, and as a result they allow withdrawals for a handful of specific reasons. You can withdraw money with no penalty to pay for college tuition and medical bills—provided, that is, your unreimbursed bills total more than 10 percent of your income. You can also take $10,000 out to be used toward the purchase of a home.

In addition, you are allowed to "borrow" your own money from a 401(k) for up to five years before you are subject to withdrawal penalties. That money can be "borrowed" for any reason. No one will be asking questions. However, that five-year borrowing period expires much sooner if you leave the job where you have the 401(k). You'll need to either repay the money within a few weeks or pay penalties on it. For obvious reasons, this can be horrible timing.

The Roth IRA offers a bit more flexibility. You can withdraw your *original contributions at any time* without penalty. But be careful! With specific exceptions, such as buying your first home or paying eligible education expenses, the earnings on those contributions need to remain in the account for at least five years and until you are over the age of fifty-nine and a half. Violate these rules, and once again the federal government will charge you for the privilege of accessing your own money.

Our advice: If you are tempted to use the money in your retirement account for a reason other than retirement, we suggest you return to the first chapter and take the "emergency" test. If it passes the emergency test and you don't have any better options, take the money. If it doesn't pass this test, don't.

And know this: The vast amount of money in retirement accounts is shielded from creditors in the event of bankruptcy. If you are in tough financial straits, it's yet another reason why it's unwise to withdraw retirement funds to partially pay down your debts. One other perk: College financial aid offices often exclude retirement accounts when determining how much a family can afford to pay for college.

IF YOU CHANGE JOBS, DON'T CHANGE RETIREMENT ACCOUNTS

If you leave your job for another one, you might believe you need to transfer your money out of your workplace retirement plan and into an IRA. You've probably seen the TV ads that encourage you to believe this. *"Your money should work as hard as you do. It's just sitting there!"* Or you're like Janie, a friend of Harold's, who called the mutual fund company servicing her plan for advice when she was changing jobs, and it told her to do it, saying she would increase her investing options if she just put the company fully in charge.

Janie got all excited. Luckily for her, she called Harold for an opinion about her new investing options before she sent the paperwork in.

Workplace retirement plans almost always come with lower-fee investment options and stronger regulatory protections than you will get on your own. Your money is *supposed* to sit there, sensibly invested, and left alone. Rollover IRAs often come with high expenses and fees that can drag down your savings over time (we'll get into this in the next few chapters).

The financial services sector has no vested interest in letting you in on this little financial fun fact. Why? It stands to gain if you roll over your workplace retirement account to it. A researcher for the Pension Policy Center recently called a number of mutual fund and insurance companies as well as banks and discovered the vast majority repeatedly told him to move his funds over to an IRA, even though he would have done better to leave the money in place.

Don't fall for stories that you can invest in more funds or that it will be easier to monitor your money if it is all in one place.

ANOTHER WAY TO SAVE: COLLEGE SAVINGS ACCOUNTS

The federal tax code also encourages people to put money aside for their children's college bills. How does that work?

There are two ways to do this. The first is called a Coverdell Education Savings Account, or ESA, and the other is called a 529 plan. Coverdell ESAs are a good starting point because they are simple and economical. If you are more affluent, pay high state taxes, or have relatives who want to chip in on special occasions, the 529 is a good bet. You can contribute to both on an after-tax basis, and then, as with an IRA or Roth IRA, the money is allowed to grow in the account tax-free. A Coverdell can be set up at a low-cost brokerage like Vanguard, while 529s are offered through the states and are easy to set up online.

Our advice? These are a great deal. Take advantage of them if you can—provided, that is, you've maxed out your retirement contributions first.

	Coverdell Education Savings Account	529 account
FEDERAL CAP ON CONTRIBUTIONS	$2,000.	Limited only by students' pertinent education costs. However, gift taxes may apply if annual contributions for a specific designated beneficiary from all sources exceed $14,000.
AGE LIMITS	Contributions must be made when your child is under eighteen or experiences special needs. Must generally be used before age thirty.	None at the federal level. Some state plans impose age restrictions.
FAMILY INCOME LIMITS	Allowed contributions phase out when modified adjusted gross income exceeds $110,000 for single filers, $220,000 for married joint filers.	None.

INVESTMENT OPTIONS	Low-fee index funds are generally available.	Vary by state, sometimes with high fees.
STATE TAX ADVANTAGES	Typically none.	Many states provide significant tax advantages for in-state plans.
DEDUCTIBLE ON YOUR CURRENT FEDERAL TAXES	No.	No.
CAN I USE FOR K-12 EXPENSES?	Yes.	No.
WHAT IF WITHDRAWALS EXCEED QUALIFIED EDUCATION EXPENSES?	Account holder pays tax (plus 10% penalty) on some portion of the withdrawals that exceed qualified educational expenses.	Account holder pays tax (plus 10% penalty) on some portion of the withdrawals that exceed qualified educational expenses.

TAKE CONTROL

Are you sensing a theme slowly emerging in these pages? If you are, it goes something like this: "This is your financial life. Take control of it."

Nowhere does this theme resonate more than in the arena of tax-advantaged savings, where so many options are at your fingertips and yet so many of us end up doing so little about it.

Rule #4:

Never Buy or Sell Individual Stocks

TO REPEAT: DO. NOT. BUY. INDIVIDUAL. STOCKS.

Harold learned everything he needed to know about investing in individual stocks growing up in Rochester, New York.

Back in the day, Rochester's leading employer was named Eastman Kodak. Maybe you've heard of it. The venerated company made film stock that was considered *the* film for cameras for most of the twentieth century. In the 1970s, the company controlled almost the entire film market in the United States. Paul Simon named a song after one of its products—Kodachrome. Kodak was so iconic, so strong, it was made part of the Dow Jones Industrial Average of thirty stocks. If there was a sure bet, that bet would be Kodak, minting those little golden boxes of film. Many of the parents of Harold's schoolmates worked at Kodak. Many had also loaded up on Kodak stock.

And then it all turned—to borrow a photographic term—negative.

First, Fujifilm and other international manufacturers discovered the film market in a big way during the 1980s. And then digital struck. Layoff after layoff roiled the iconic company and its hometown. The Dow Jones delisted the company in 2004. In 2012, the company declared bankruptcy. Oh, but surely, you think, I would have known to dump the stock in time. Or I would have recognized the film market had serious issues before I lost my retirement savings.

Maybe. You might not have thought to get out at the top, but you likely would have sold before you completely lost everything. But then again, we all think we're the person who would have bought Apple in 1980.

More likely, we'd be Harold's family friend Miriam.

Miriam was watching a lot of television in those days. Week in and week out, she heard respectable people on PBS name this stock and that stock, saying it was a sure thing. (This was before CNBC.) She almost certainly heard the legendary investor Peter Lynch's philosophy that when it came to stocks, a good place to go looking for investments was the products and stores you know, use, and love.

Miriam's family used to eat at a local pizzeria, which was expanding to other locations. The pizza was first-rate. The joint was always packed. This was not your random corner pizzeria. It was special. It was going places.

So when franchising that local pizzeria went public, Miriam, along with many other local customers, invested a chunk of her savings. Kodak wasn't working out for them, but pizza sure would—or so they thought. For a time, it was a great ride. The pizzeria invited all stockholders, no matter how small, to the annual shareholders meeting. It was a heck of a lot of fun. Their wonderful "Any way you want it" pizza, lasagna, and all manner of goodies would be served. Rumors abounded that Sbarro or some other large chain was interested in buying in. The stock went up and up.

Because the title of this chapter is "Never Buy or Sell Individual Stocks," you can guess where this is going. The buyout never happened. That local pizzeria is still in business, but the franchising stock is almost worthless. The last Harold heard, the company had one employee, whose "duties do not require his full-time attention."

Miriam thought she was investing in a sure winner. Instead, she invested in a long shot that didn't pan out.

So you think this won't happen to you? It was the 1980s, after all. Well, think again.

Helaine would like it noted that when it comes to investing in individual companies, she's Miriam.

Way back in the late 1990s, Helaine spent quite a bit of time thinking about investing. She was, after all, editing the Money Makeover personal finance feature at the *Los Angeles Times*. But the late 1990s was the time of the dot-com boom. Everyone was sure this was the one. All you had to do was purchase the right techy blue chip, watch it ascend into the stratosphere, and *ka-ching!* And picking it—wow, that was easy. Anyone could do it.

And for a time, that was actually true. That's the thing about bubbles and great market runs. Anyone can make money.

Until times change or the bubble bursts.

Helaine knew better. Helaine tried very hard to be the

voice of common sense. Week in and week out, she told families who turned to the newspaper for help with their finances the same thing. Most of us don't have the ability to really do this stock-picking thing very well. Whatever you do, stay away from individual stocks—especially if they are less than five or ten years old. They have no track record. Most of these companies are showing nothing in the way of profit.

But . . . it was so tempting.

There were two companies Helaine had more than a passing familiarity with that went public in those years. Amazon and AOL.

Let's just say she decided to invest in the one that brought you the memorable catchphrase "You've got mail."

What's the moral of the story? Yes, mutual and exchange-traded funds are better. But even more important—one more time and this time with feeling—*do not buy individual stocks.*

YOU'RE NOT WARREN BUFFETT

We all like to think that given enough time and discipline, we can all become Warren Buffett. You know who Warren Buffett is, right? He's the legendary stock picker who is widely considered one of the most astute sages of investing in our lifetime. Known for his pithy, folksy wisdom—"Never ask a barber if you need a haircut"; "When the tide goes out, you discover who's been swimming naked"—he's considered the ultimate stock guru by people who often forget to mention that not only is he an excellent stock picker but he also benefits from getting access to deals not available to mere run-of-the-mill investors like, well, the rest of us.

Many individual investors believe that *they* have the potential to be Warren Buffett. When people experience this delusion, we like to refer them to the work of the behavioral finance stars Brad Barber and Terrance Odean at the University of California. No, they aren't household names, which is too bad. They have not written bestselling books of investment advice. Instead, they have devoted their careers to demonstrating the folly of the individual investor.

Their papers demonstrate—over and over again—that when it comes to making investment decisions, if we are guaranteed to do one thing, it's to make the wrong call. We believe we are out in front of trends when, in fact, we are chasing them. We buy when the market is going up and sell when it is going down, which is a great way of locking in losses and making less money over time. We panic. The stocks we buy perform notably *worse* than the stocks we sell. We have, as Helaine frequently notes, a black thumb when it comes to stock picking and investing.

Don't get us wrong. People do hit the occasional home run. Yet studies suggest that less than 1 percent of us have the ability to consistently and regularly beat the Street.

Instead of trying to beat the Street, we would all be better off just trying to keep up with it. We'll talk in the next chapter about the way to achieve this. For right now, know this: Not only will individual stock picking not lead you to beat the market, but it will likely leave you behind— possibly way behind.

"But, but, but?" we hear you asking. Why would brokerage houses sponsor classes in learning about active trading and options? If it's not in my best interests, why would they claim they can teach me how to do it?

Well, they have an incentive to get you to act in ways that are not in your best financial interest. Hundreds of millions of them, in fact. When you trade or make bets on the market via their platforms, they make money by charging you for each and every trade. Whether you win or lose is irrelevant. You still need to pay to play.

By the way, Warren Buffett doesn't want his own heirs to invest like Warren Buffett. He probably knows that he can get special terms because he is Warren Buffett. Instead, he wants them to invest in . . . well, we'll tell you in the next chapter.

FINANCIAL ADVISORS DON'T PLAY THIS GAME MUCH BETTER THAN YOU DO (THOUGH THEY CHARGE YOU TO PLAY IT) AND MIGHT EVEN BE WORSE

Many people look at behavioral finance as a way they can learn to outsmart the markets. They are convinced they can teach themselves to be more rational if they know the irrational fears they could fall prey to. Financial advisors even market themselves this way: I know the behavioral quirks, so I can avoid them for you. "You might not be able to pick stocks, but I most certainly can" is how the pitch goes. When Helaine wrote *Pound Foolish,* she found marketing experts and even academic behavioral finance stars who told financial advisors to say such things.

Any five-minute reading of a behavioral finance expert tells you that this is unlikely. Many financial advisors can offer valuable insights for a variety of life situations. What they *do not* offer is superior expertise picking stocks. As the financial journalist Felix Salmon put it, "Trying to pick a winning money manager is even more of a losing game than trying to pick a winning stock." Why? For starters, financial advisors are, like all humans, prey to their own biases. One of the most important biases is the overconfidence that comes with expertise. If anything, their overconfidence and sometimes their skewed incentives can even lead them more astray.

One other thing we learn from behavioral science: Men tend to achieve lower returns than women. It's not because the ladies are better at stock picking. Rather, women are better at *not* picking stocks than men. As a result, ladies trade less, saving money on investment fees and boosting their returns. Your great advantage as an investor is that you can be boring and methodical, rising with the overall market and not wasting money on costly trading that tends to underperform the market.

NO ONE ON TV (OR THE INTERNET) KNOWS A STOCK'S FUTURE

Harold blames many of our woes on a man he considers the world's greatest villain: Louis Rukeyser. Okay, he really wasn't the world's greatest villain. But he gave bad advice.

You probably don't remember Rukeyser. Once, in the pre-cable, pre-Internet era, the avuncular, well-spoken, middle-aged man hosted an erudite show on PBS about the week in the stock market called *Wall Street Week*. For years, this was Harold's friend Miriam's favorite show.

Rukeyser did not come off as a charlatan or tacky TV huckster. He was no evangelist espousing the gospel of wealth. He didn't clown around or shout like many TV pitchmen. He wasn't a cable TV sex symbol. Instead, he was a calm voice of authority. Week in and week out, Rukeyser and his guests would give investment advice, complete with their favorite stock picks. They would try to predict where the Dow Jones Industrial Average was going over the next year.

In its gentle way, *Wall Street Week* spread the toxic message that playing the stocks is easy and fun. And the professorial Rukeyser looked downright responsible compared with screaming banshees on cable TV financial shows like Jim Cramer or anonymous tweeters sharing information on the Web.

CNBC's entire business model is based on encouraging individual stock picking. CEOs come on to discuss why viewers should invest in their companies. Analysts appear, discussing bank recommendations and sells. "You need to get in the game!" shouts the manic *Mad Money* host, Jim Cramer, day in and day out, as he barks out his "expert" analysis of individual stocks.

How well does this work?

While we were writing this chapter, the website Zero Hedge pointed us to a delightful example: GT Advanced Technologies. The company manufactured a component that would be used in the iPhone 6. "Talk about growth," Cramer exclaimed on his show in August 2014. How could it go wrong? Easily, sad to report. Less than two months later, the company filed for bankruptcy, and the stock price plunged to less than $1.

It happened a lot faster than Kodak's bankruptcy.

Yeah, we know. "How Jim Cramer gets it wrong" could be filed under the subject heading "Shooting Fish in a Barrel." One academic analysis found the best way to make money off his show was to immediately short (that is, bet against) any stock he screams viewers should buy. That's not totally because Cramer doesn't get the fundamentals, by the way. It's because a viewer might think he (and it is almost always "he," Helaine would remind everyone) and Cramer have an intimate, one-to-one relationship. In fact, at least fifty thousand people are watching the show at any moment. A decent proportion will sometimes run out and buy the stock at once. Its price correspondingly rises and then, often, crashes back down to earth.

But Jim Cramer is no different from anyone else. Sure, he's famous, but there are literally hundreds of names you can substitute for his and not know the difference. The Internet abounds with people and organizations offering supposedly sage stock advice. There's *The Motley Fool* and *Seeking Alpha* and StockTwits, where individuals sign up and give their thumbs-ups or thumbs-downs in 140-character tweets. There are newsletters clogging up in-boxes, missives that claim to predict decades of booming growth or a twenty-five-year depression. (Don't believe it? Just check Helaine's in-box.) Financial advisors and wealth managers and stockbrokers will pitch you, too, claiming some special insight on the market.

Or you can turn to the conference circuit, which ranges from high-end events like the Sohn Investment Conference, where attendees pay thousands of dollars to hear the latest plays from hedge fund superstars like David Einhorn and Bill Ackman, to free-to-the-public events like the World MoneyShow, where exhibitors ranging from respectable

Fidelity Investments to obvious quacks pitch their wares at the mostly over-sixty-five crowd.

They all have some version of the same story. They can teach you to understand company and market fundamentals. Once provided with this esoteric knowledge, you, too, can read the tea leaves of the market and make money. And how do you get the information? Why, you pay for it, of course.

Whether high-gloss *Wall Street Week,* slightly crazy Jim Cramer, hyper up-to-the-second tweet, or some conference marketing dubious financial products or newsletters to senior citizens, it's all the same damaging message: Playing the stock market is easy and fun. The smart investor is someone who can pick a good stock or anticipate the market.

Not true.

The ideal advice show or convention or podcast would always start with someone's reading aloud the index card that comes with this book. That would be boring to watch or listen to week after week, even on PBS. No one would pay to go to a conference featuring speaker after speaker promoting that viewpoint. No one would buy that newsletter. And that's kind of the point. The less you think about such individual companies, the better.

No matter how much you study, no matter how much you learn, you will never be clairvoyant. And neither will anyone else. There are no market psychics out there. Not even on TLC.

YOU'RE NOT A BILLIONAIRE, AND YOU CAN'T INVEST LIKE ONE

Let's say you are someone who believes there is a way to predict the future of the stock market and any common stock.

Here's one thing Harold and Helaine have learned in a combined one hundred years on the planet: It's hard to change how people think. So for this one section of the book, we are going to play along with you. Out there, in the great wide world, there is someone on television, someone on the Internet, someone at one of those stock market shows and conventions, who has it all figured out.

Question: Are you a billionaire?

That's a rhetorical question. We're not either. So why are we asking you?

We want you to use your common sense when thinking about investments.

You are a regular person. You have some money. You earn a decent living. But you aren't on the *Forbes* list of the hundred wealthiest human beings.

Now pretend Helaine is a stock market guru bearing tips. And let's say she's the real thing.

Why would Helaine be sharing her insights with you? Wouldn't common sense say to take her act to someone worth billions of dollars so she could invest her way to billions too? Or, alternately, why tell anyone at all? Would you really go through the effort of promoting your gizmo, sweating every $5,000 conference attendee or $700 computerized stock market predictor sale or $199 stock buy?

Or would you move to a tax-free tropical isle and spend your days trading successfully via your satellite Wi-Fi connection on board your yacht?

This question answers itself.

In other words, the person promoting the stock or the investment has something to gain by persuading you to think a certain way. And you might not ever know why. You know how you avoid that problem?

Yes, we are going to say it again. Don't buy individual stocks.

ALTERNATIVE INVESTMENTS: NOT NEARLY
AS FUN AS ALTERNATIVE LIFESTYLES

If you are contemplating the individual investing route, you are also leaving yourself open to people marketing so-called alternative investments. Their appeals will often sound, well . . . appealing. *Bitcoin is going to be the new alternative currency! Get in on it now!* Or whatever.

Alternative investments essentially mean any investment that's not a stock, a bond, cash, or real estate. Even the most out-there stock purchase is not considered an alternative investment. On the other hand, purchasing the *Mona Lisa* would be considered an alternative investment.

What could go wrong?

A lot.

"Alternative" is not, like in music, simply an excuse to go to the desert, hold a festival, and get high. It's a nice way of saying "This is a really risky investment that is hard to transparently value and that is subject to great swings in price."

You don't need to learn what a European call option is and how it differs from an American one. If you knew, that knowledge would provide zero help to you as you devise a sensible savings plan.

Gold is an especially popular investment for those predicting imminent apocalypse. You'll need it—its prophets say—when oil runs out or when a cyber hacker destroys our economic system. Well, maybe. But ask yourself this: How long do you think you will be allowed to live in peace in this postapocalyptic world once word gets around your neighborhood about the gold you have stashed in the basement?

Others will push collectibles, things like art and stamps. Or maybe investing in films and Broadway shows. They serve a double—nay, triple—purpose. You get to enjoy the hobby, show it off to your friends, and still make money.

Collectibles come with their own volatility. Today's hot young artist has the potential to be tomorrow's has-been. One year, antiques from the American colonial period are in, and then the tide turns and everyone wants Le Corbusier, whom Harold has never heard of. Then there are the trends and manias, like Beanie Babies.

Our advice: Collect stamps, coins, or Beanie Babies if that's your passion. Don't treat these hobbies as investments that will pay off someday. It's unlikely they ever will.

The bigger point is this: Alternative investments tend to be highly subject to trends, manias, and erratic or dramatic price swings. They bring unpredictability into your life. You don't need that.

BUY AND HOLD 'EM

Finally, buying individual stocks encourages trading, which will not only erode your profits in transaction costs but also encourage you to do all the wrong things with your investments. When you invest in individual stocks, you are essentially trying to time the market. You are trying to buy assets when they are undervalued, holding on until they run up in price.

Once again, you—or anyone else—is highly unlikely to figure this all out and still come out ahead when accounting for transaction costs.

But it goes deeper. You might believe that you are a calm and rational investor. But when we invest in individual stocks, we are not engaging—no matter what we think—in prudent, reasonable investments. We are speculating. You may be researching your stocks and investing with caution and care. It doesn't matter. No matter what the financial services industry would like you to believe, most of the time you are a more respectable version of someone playing poker or craps in Vegas.

Even if you devote your days and nights to this, it's unlikely you can foresee and react properly to every change in consumer whims, every unexpected event, executive shake-up, or all the other factors that can affect an individual company.

So what makes sense?

Buy and hold a small selection of indexed mutual or exchange-traded funds for the long haul.

This is a tough-love moment for some of you. It's a bummer to give up on the prospect of a big win. Everyone knows of someone who knows someone who knows someone who bought Apple in 1991 and made a bundle. Relatives and friends tend to mention such things. They don't tend to mention the $5,000 they plunked down on Pets .com. It would be really fun to pick the right stock and get really rich.

But for others, this should actually come as a huge relief. You might be thinking, "I don't have to do all this stuff— watch business news, constantly monitor my investments— in order to get ahead?" Indeed you don't. Once you realize that stock picking is a loser's game, you can get on with the rest of your life without feeling guilty about it.

There's no good reason to miss a child's bedtime story or an evening out with friends so you can read Facebook's annual report. There's no good reason to let something slide on your day job because you are working on your investments either. Your time is valuable. Your happiness and economic security depend on your marriage, your family, your success at work and in your relationships. Investments in those areas are almost certain to pay off.

Rule #5:

Buy Inexpensive, Well-Diversified Indexed Mutual Funds and Exchange-Traded Funds

INVEST YOUR SAVINGS

So you've made sure to sign up for your 401(k). Or there is money you have lingering in a private brokerage account and it's invested in whatever the heck a financial advisor suggested. Now you are ready to grapple with it.

But what exactly should you do with your money? You signed up for a subscription to a well-respected financial magazine, but it seems to be recommending a different "best" mutual fund every month. That's no help.

Helaine would like to report that the first job she took that offered a defined contribution plan, she promptly took all the papers over to her father-in-law. He filled them out, and she signed her name. She has no memory of what she invested in.

Harold's early investing was equally thought-out and informed. Thinking back to his first job, he can't recall anything about his initial retirement funding paperwork. He certainly did nothing with it; he saved precisely nothing for the next two years. Then a colleague with a side interest in finance mentioned it. Harold was initially skeptical and lazy, but the colleague kept pushing it, and Harold signed up, mostly to get the colleague to stop haranguing him about this boring financial stuff. For the remaining year he worked there, he put aside $2,500 with the company match. He randomly invested the money in two of the offered options and never gave it much thought again.

This sort of behavior is not uncommon. Most of us ignore this stuff or invest our savings in such a haphazard way it almost seems like a misuse of the word "investment" to describe how we handle our nest eggs. We know it. We've done it ourselves. We've heard stories over the years of people who check off all the investment options open to them in their retirement plans, because they can't decide or they assume they all must be okay if their company offers them.

As we discovered, there are only a few simple rules you need to learn to take on the challenge of investing and build yourself an easy, basic, and all-weather portfolio. Oh, and knowledge of a few terms helps too.

NOT ALL MUTUAL FUNDS ARE CREATED EQUAL

Let's start with mutual funds.

Mutual funds are, at their base, the pooled money of hundreds of thousands of investors. Most mutual funds have a professional manager who is actively involved in selecting the investments for the fund. This is called—wait for it—active management. He decides, say, that Apple is going to go up in price faster than Microsoft or that interest rates on bonds are going to suddenly rise, and he makes purchases on behalf of the fund accordingly.

It certainly sounds kosher, right? The managers are professionals, after all. They've been doing this full-time for years, often decades in fact. They aren't—like you—poring over lists of stocks and bonds at 9:30 p.m., after a long day of work when almost anyone would rather be lying on a couch binge watching Netflix. They aren't surreptitiously checking an online dictionary to figure out the difference between value and growth. They are highly trained and highly paid experts on different economic sectors.

This is certainly the impression the industry would like you to have. T. Rowe Price, for example, says its expertise allows you to "invest with confidence."

> *How could a luminous protein in jellyfish impact life expectancy in the U.S., real estate in Hong Kong, and the optics industry in Germany? At T. Rowe Price, we understand the connections of a complex global economy.*

Wow—they really understand all that?

Well, it would be nice to believe that. Unfortunately, that's not so. According to a recent survey, over a five-year period more than 80 percent of domestic stock funds performed worse than the market index they were set up to surpass. The results were slightly better for funds specializing in international investments. They underperformed only more than 50 percent of the time. As if this were not enough, almost 25 percent of all mutual funds merged with others or closed entirely during this period.

Why don't they do better? Well, remember the last chapter, when we told you all about how practically no one is successful at picking stocks over the long run? We explained how it didn't matter if they went on CNBC or wrote a newsletter or popular blog or were simply your supposedly talented cousin.

You can add mutual fund manager to that list.

As it turns out, being more educated or having more letters or credentials after your name or having the important-sounding job of managing a mutual fund doesn't make anyone more immune from the pitfalls and pratfalls of investing. It doesn't make anyone trade less or hold on to stocks longer. It doesn't keep anyone from falling prey to investing biases. It doesn't stop anyone from panicking or allowing overconfidence in his or her ability to sway them.

The result? Research has repeatedly shown that less than 1 percent of actively managed funds were able to beat the index they were set up to surpass when trading and other expenses were taken into account. A recent *New York Times* article brutally summarized current evidence: "Who

Routinely Trounces the Stock Market? Try 2 out of 2,862 Funds."

FOLLOW WARREN BUFFETT'S ADVICE:
INVEST IN INDEX FUNDS

Many people look to the wisdom of Warren Buffett. There are lots of conferences and books devoted to teaching individual investors to channel their inner Warren Buffett, but clearly Warren Buffett doesn't think much of them. How do we know this? Well, a few years ago, the now-octogenarian Buffett published a letter to his two sons and one daughter saying how he thought they should invest when he was no longer here. His suggestion? "A very low-cost S&P 500 index fund."

Index funds are pegged to match a particular benchmark, and the stocks in the fund are selected and maintained to that standard. It might be the S&P 500 or the Wilshire 5000 Total Market Index. It could be a bond index like a government bond index or a high-yield one.

An index fund doesn't seek to do better than the index it is meant to replicate. On the other hand, it won't do worse. That, it turns out, is the magic investing formula. It's the opposite of active management. It's passive management.

BEWARE OF FEES

Index funds also do better for their investor because the actual cost of investing in one is less than investing in a managed fund.

When you invest your hard-earned money in a mutual fund or any investment for that matter, it's not a freebie, no matter what financial salespeople claim.

Think of your investment for a moment as you would a home. As with owning a house, you have to pay bills for maintenance. But instead of having the gutters cleaned and the windows washed, you pay the people running mutual funds for research, trading costs, and advertising. The management serves as a sort of contractor for the mutual fund.

And like conventional contractors, some financial services companies pad the bill more than others. Index funds are the equivalent of the no-frills renovation. They don't have to employ armies of researchers. They use computer programs to adjust the investment to stay even with the index. As a result, while the average annual fee for a managed stock mutual fund is 0.89 percent, the average fee for an equity index fund is a much more reasonable 0.12 percent.

Those numbers sure don't sound like much. It's only a

0.77 percent difference. Well, when it comes to investing expenses, remember a corny early 1960s love song: Little things mean a lot.

Let's look at this simple example. You're going to choose between putting a onetime $5,000 investment in one of two mutual funds. We'll call them Strawberry and Orange. The underlying investments will grow at 6 percent annually, and you will leave it there for thirty years. The actively managed fund is Strawberry, and it charges the average fee of 0.89 percent. Orange, the index fund, charges 0.12 percent.

Management fee	Amount in your account thirty years from now
Orange 0.12%	$27,758
Strawberry 0.89%	$22,299

That's a difference of more than $5,000. And this is by no means an extreme comparison. If you look in the newspaper, you will find well-known actively managed funds that charge much more than we assume.

Now, yes, if those fees produced greater and more reliable returns, they would be worth it. But they don't. They are only enriching the financial services sector at the expense of your own bottom line. Robert Hiltonsmith, a researcher at the think tank Demos, has estimated that the average household loses $155,000 in potential gains as a result of unnecessary fees.

NOT ALL INDEX FUND FAMILIES ARE CREATED EQUAL

So put your money in an index fund and all will be fine? Not exactly. It would be nice if we could assume that any index fund comes with the lowest and best expense ratio. Unfortunately, this isn't true. Take Vanguard's flagship fund, the Vanguard 500 Index Fund. It has a lovely and low expense ratio of 0.17 percent. On the other hand, many index funds charge 0.7 percent, and some even more. Sometimes they soar to more than 1 percent. And no, it's not significantly more expensive to run one index fund than another. The difference fattens the bottom line of the offending financial services firm offering the more expensive fund.

These fees really add up. We can't repeat it enough.

So why do the firms selling these costly funds continue to charge so much? Answer: because they can. In some cases, it's because the funds are provided in a 401(k), and if you want to invest in an index fund in your retirement account, that option may not be available in your company's plan. Unfortunately you can't, after all, invest in another company's 401(k). It's not a competitive situation for the investor. As Helaine once put it in an article, "It's not like you were shopping for a blazer at Saks Fifth Avenue, looked at the price tag, and decided to go across the street to Zara instead. Unless you get a new job, you are stuck."

In other cases, the financial firms offering the investments just think their customers will allow them to get away with higher fees, and, clearly, because they have customers, they are correct.

MUTUAL FUNDS VERSUS EXCHANGE-TRADED FUNDS

There are two ways to invest in index funds. The first is via a mutual fund. The second is what is called an exchange-traded fund (ETF). What's the difference?

- Mutual funds are not always index funds. Exchange-traded funds are almost always pegged to an index or other benchmark.

- Exchange-traded funds can be traded like stocks. Mutual funds can be bought and sold only at the end of the business day.

- Exchange-traded funds almost always have lower expense ratios but higher trading costs than mutual funds.

What's better? We can't really answer that one. It really depends on your personal circumstances and preferences, not to mention what is available in your workplace retirement plan. But one thing is clear: If the ability to buy and sell your investment at all times of the day is important to you, you have bigger issues. (See Rule #4.) That advice goes double for mutual funds and ETFs. The only people making money in this scenario are the financial firms receiving the trading commissions.

HOW TO INVEST

The phrase "asset allocation" is one of those narcolepsy-inducing insider terms that is much more complicated sounding than it is. It almost seems designed to make sure a huge number of people want nothing to do with this complex investing thing, not to mention allowing financial advisors to sound important while doling out very basic advice.

So what is it exactly?

Different types of investments can be classified into different categories. A well-designed portfolio will contain representatives of several of them, with proportions determined by such factors as age, long-term investing goals, and risk tolerance. This is called diversification.

We diversify to spread risk. The idea is that not everything in your investment portfolio rises and falls by the same amount at the same time. By not putting all your eggs in one basket, you protect yourself against any one investment's misfortune. You also, to the extent possible, protect yourself against larger, systemic risks that may affect various sectors of the economy.

If you quickly scan the Internet, you will see that there are people out there who say if you go this route, you need at least ten funds to achieve proper diversification. There are mid-caps and real estate investment trusts and international small caps, and maybe you should do one or two managed funds to hedge against downturns and . . . MAKE IT STOP.

If you are reading this book, you are almost certainly in search of simplicity. (Perhaps that's why you were attracted to a book with the words "Index Card" in the title.) We are trying to make things simple for you.

Most of us don't need a complicated, elaborately planned investment scheme that requires more choices and frequent changes. As the cliché goes, don't let the perfect be the enemy of the good. There is no perfect investment scheme anyway. Don't let anyone tell you otherwise.

Are we guaranteeing success or protecting you from every bad scenario? No. That's not possible. Instead, we're offering you a simple, easy-to-follow action plan.

So how do you sort all this out?

Portfolios are traditionally organized by age, what you need the money for, and whether your risk tolerance is high, low, or somewhere in between. They are also—for the most part—divided between stocks and bonds.

A stock is a share in a publicly traded company. A bond, on the other hand, is a loan to a company. In return for the loan, the company promises to both pay interest on the money given to it and pay the loan—that is, the bond—back by a certain specified date. As a result, many people consider a bond a more stable investment than a stock, which can go up and down in value, with no guaranteed return. On the other hand, stocks tend to do better over time than bonds.

The sooner you think you need the money, the less risk

you should assume. If you have a pot of money put aside to buy a house, and you are planning to purchase it this year, you should probably move it into a short-term bond fund. The same is true for your emergency money. Never make the assumption that a stock market that is going up will continue to go up until the day you need the money. Nobody can predict these short-term movements. Occasionally, the stock market has a really bad day. On six occasions since 1997, the stock market dropped by 7 percent or more *in a single day*. (Okay, one of these times was only 6.98 percent. It was still a very bad day.) Other times, it has a very bad year—it declined by 34 percent in 2008. You don't want that to happen to the money set aside for your daughter's college tuition this fall.

Conversely, if you are twenty-five years old and this is your retirement savings, an aggressive growth strategy is likely better. The healthier and wealthier you are, the more risks you can reasonably take. Why? You have time to recover from setbacks. Moreover, if you are in your twenties or thirties, you are probably not in your prime earning years, meaning your household income is likely to increase, allowing you to compensate for any investing losses.

Finally, you can be saving and investing money for any

number of reasons. You could be investing for your retirement or saving up to buy your first home. It could be college savings or a dream vacation. It might be your emergency savings. It might be something to help your kids.

So how do you determine how much money you should put in stock market funds versus bond funds? Well, conventional advice goes something like this:

1. What's your age?
2. Subtract that number from 100.
3. The answer is the percentage of your assets that should be invested in stocks.

There are now financial sages out there who say you should up the base number from 100 to 110. That's what Harold is doing. This advice, needless to say, comes with the assumption that all this money is targeted for your retirement.

Something else worth noting: This formula assumes stocks will perform better than bonds over the long haul. That is indeed the conventional wisdom. Since 1928, the S&P stock index has returned a premium of about 6 percent above what one could receive from safe government bonds.

Case closed? Not exactly. First, this is a very long period of time to hold stocks. Second, this ignores the first rule of investing: Past performance is no guarantee of future returns. The U.S. stock market did indeed perform quite well in the twentieth century. It might happen again. But it might not.

What do we think? Well, perhaps it is helpful to discuss how Helaine deals with this dilemma. A lot of people read *Pound Foolish,* where she discusses it at some length, and ask her where in her backyard she buries her savings. The answer: at a discount brokerage, invested in a fairly sensible way. Why? She has no faith in her ability to guess the future. Most people who question conventional wisdom are fairly certain they can outsmart everyone else. Helaine believes it is quite possible she could get it wrong. Think of it this way: The stock market can go down 20 percent while your chosen alternative crashes 40 percent.

Ironically, playing things too safe brings its own risks. If you put money only in supersafe assets that earn correspondingly low returns, such as a bank savings account, you'll increase your risk of outliving your money, not to mention actually losing money relative to inflation.

Given that nobody can predict the future, here's a sensible investment portfolio for a forty-year-old. This investor's bond allocation is 40 percent because we recommend that your bond allocation roughly equal your age.

60% STOCKS	70% S&P index fund	42%
	15% small-cap index fund	9%
	15% international fund	9%
40% BONDS	100% long term	40%
TOTAL		100%

For your stock investments, we suggest:

Seventy percent: A good S&P 500 index fund. This fund will provide domestic and international (more on that later) exposure to large-cap companies based in the United States. The S&P 500 represents industries that include technology, banking, and health care so you are assured quick diversification.

Fifteen percent: A small-cap index fund such as the Russell 2000 Index. While large-cap companies tend to drive headlines, you also want to make sure your portfolio contains exposure to small-cap funds. Why? Small-cap funds have generally outperformed large-cap funds. Before we get too excited about outperformance, remember that it comes with greater risk. Think of small-cap companies as small and agile. Some companies will be poised for growth and may even evolve into large-cap companies, while others may go bust. You will see this in the slightly more volatile returns of small-cap companies.

Fifteen percent: A broad-based international fund like Vanguard's Total International Stock Index Fund. You will want an international fund that has access to both developed—think Europe and parts of Asia—and emerging—think South America, Africa, and other parts of Asia—markets. Make sure that you choose an international fund and not a "global" fund. An international fund will have little to no holdings in U.S.-based companies, whereas a global fund will try to mimic the globe and, in turn, have exposure to the United States.

At first glance, a 15 percent allocation to international markets may seem small in our increasingly globalized world. However, you still get exposure to international markets through the S&P 500 index fund. In fact, in 2013, Goldman Sachs found that foreign sales accounted for 33 percent of S&P 500 revenue. When you think about companies like Coca-Cola, Apple, and Nike, the numbers make sense.

If that's too complicated for you, you can replace the S&P 500 index fund and the small-cap fund with one total stock market index fund. That's an all-encompassing fund, representing the entirety of the domestic stock market.

As for bonds, once again, you don't need to go out and research individual offerings from companies, not to mention all sorts of governing authorities ranging from the U.S. Treasury to local municipal construction projects. A long-term bond index fund will suffice. This is a fund where the bonds have a minimum maturity of ten years. The thirty-year Treasury bond is a classic long-term bond.

Long-term bonds almost always offer higher interest rates than short-term bonds—that is, bonds with the due date less than five years away. Why? Investors require a premium for tying up their money for such a long period, during which the available interest rates on competing investments might rise. Now, of course, if you invest via a mutual or exchange-traded fund, you aren't tying up your money; you can sell off your investment at any time.

Finally, if you don't own a house, condo, or other property, you might want to consider putting a small percentage—maybe 5 to 10 percent—of your money into a real estate investment trust index fund, also known as a REIT. This allows you to own investments in office buildings, hotels, apartment buildings, shopping malls, and other forms of real estate. This allocation can come from your bond holdings.

TARGET-DATE FUNDS ARE NOT GUARANTEES

Then there is the life-cycle fund, often better known as a target-date fund. They come with names like Total Retirement 2030.

Life-cycle funds originated about twenty years ago. The thought behind them was good: It would be a one-stop investment for people who either weren't savvy or didn't want to think much about their retirement funds. Today, if you are automatically diverted into a 401(k) plan, the chances are quite good you've been defaulted into a target-date fund.

These funds promise the ultimate in simplicity—one fund for all your retirement needs. It's alluring . . . so alluring that even Harold fell for it and praised it on the original index card. But Helaine and the financial expert Burton Malkiel, author of the classic *A Random Walk down Wall Street,* convinced Harold that this recommendation was wrong.

So what's the problem?

First, as it turns out, many target-date funds are surprisingly high-fee investments. The overall expense ratios are often similar to actively managed funds, although a simple target-date fund can easily be made by blending a few indexes. The financial services sector claims the additional fees are a sad but necessary by-product of making sure investors are safely on the path to retirement. They have a point. But Helaine, like a lot of other observers of the financial scene, believes something else is afoot. Because many investors in target-date funds are being defaulted into them, they are also the sorts of people who don't look too closely at the fees being charged. As a result, the average target-date fund charges about 1 percent per year, a significant boost over an index fund expense.

Moreover, surveys show that a majority of investors in target-date funds are under the impression that the fund is a guarantee—that, at a minimum, they will receive their initial investment back at all times. This is simply untrue.

DON'T MAKE YOURSELF CRAZY: KEEP INVESTING SIMPLE

Finally, we should point out that the strategies we propose are supported by solid research on financial markets, are designed for long-run investment, and don't take much time or expertise to execute given your busy life.

Almost all of us have things we want to do besides obsessively monitoring investments. We have families and pets we love and friends we want to spend time with. There are books we want to read and movies and television shows we want to watch. We suggest a sensible strategy for long-run investing. The portfolio we recommend doesn't take much time to set up and maintain. You can check it out once a year, when you are doing your taxes. That lets you tend to the parts of your life that matter the most.

Rule #6:

Make Your Financial Advisor Commit to the Fiduciary Standard

SEEKING FINANCIAL ADVICE?
LEARN THIS WORD FIRST

Harold's friend Karen once boasted to him that she didn't pay any fees to her financial advisor.

KAREN: *The funds where he invests my money take care of all that.*

HAROLD: *Oh, what funds are those?*

KAREN: *I'm not exactly sure. There are so many. He moves my money between them when he feels some sector isn't doing well. He outperforms the market by 2 to 3 percentage points, and the funds pay his fees.*

Must we tell you that Karen's investments carry high fees? And that her broker likely gets paid every time he moves her in or out of an investment?

Almost all of us believe that when we sit down to receive financial advice, the person we meet with—no matter who this person is—is duty-bound to act in our best interests:

- Eighty-seven percent of us believe that if we speak with someone affiliated with our workplace retirement plan about our overall investment portfolio, he or she is obliged to give investment advice in our best interests.

- Seventy-six percent of us believe anyone going by the designation "financial advisor" is obliged to give investment advice in our best interests.

- Sixty percent of us believe insurance agents are obliged to make recommendations based on our best interests.

Luckily, there's a simple word that can help you find good financial advice. This word is so powerful that the vast majority of the financial services industry would rather you not know it. This word lets you know if the people or companies you sought out for financial advice have a duty to put your best interests first, or if, alternately, they can prioritize their own bottom line at the expense of your own.

This word is "fiduciary."

THE FIDUCIARY STANDARD VERSUS
THE SUITABILITY STANDARD

A fiduciary is a financial advisor who has a legal and regulatory duty to put your interests ahead of his or her own.

A financial advisor working to the fiduciary standard

1. has a legal duty to act in your best interests; and
2. is not getting paid to steer you into buying overpriced investment products you don't want or need.

A majority of men and women offering financial advice don't work to the fiduciary standard. Instead, they work to something called the suitability standard. The best way to describe this standard is to say that it's the "it's okay if it's basically okay" standard for care.

How does this work in practice? Well, let's pretend you are shopping for a dress to wear to a friend's wedding. If you went to a store where the saleswoman was working to the fiduciary standard, she would have to ask you where you planned to wear the outfit. She'd inquire about your budget. As for the actual outfit itself? It would need to be flattering, the right color and fit for you. If it needed alterations, a nearby tailor could perform them inexpensively.

Now let's say you go to the store where the salespeople need to meet the suitability standard. The saleswoman is under no obligation to find you the best deal. The dress she finds might be a little too big. She might recommend a dress that needs significant and expensive alterations. She could recommend one item over another because she receives a larger commission and not tell you. She's probably not an evil person. She wants you to look good. But her advice is influenced by her own bottom line.

This is all legal. She provided adequate or suitable service.

Yes, we know we all shop for clothes that way. But, well, that's clothing. Make a mistake, and you are out maybe $50.

Financial advice, on the other hand, is all-important. Make a mistake, and you could be living with the consequences for the rest of your life. And the worst part of that? You might not even know you could have done better.

You are unlikely to ever find out that the person you believe is giving you the best, most objective financial advice on how to handle your life savings is actually steering you toward investments that are more likely to boost his bottom line than your own. Why? He doesn't need to tell you. There is no requirement that someone working to the suitability standard inform you that there is a higher standard out there or that he is receiving a significant sales bonus for steering clients toward one investment over another that would cost the customer less.

THE ONLY CREDENTIAL THAT MATTERS: FIDUCIARY

At last count, there were more than two hundred titles would-be financial consiglieri can use to convey knowledge, integrity, and expertise to their customers. There are "chartered college planning specialists" and "retirement management analysts." Merrill Lynch now has "trusted financial advisors," a title presumably meant to distinguish them from all those less-than-trustworthy financial advisors at the brokerage. And according to the Consumer Financial Protection Bureau, there are more than fifty designations designed to indicate expertise in the financial matters of senior citizens alone.

Many of these terms are about as official as "designated driver," designed mainly to make someone sound important and increase their sales of everything from annuities to estate-planning tools. There are "senior experts" and "registered senior investment advisors." Something called an accredited retirement advisor requires zero in the way of course work and has no accreditation status whatsoever.

As for the popular and common term "financial advisor," it means precisely nothing. Whether "advisor" is spelled with an *e* or an *o*, it still doesn't matter.

None of these designations contain the word "salesperson" or "broker," but that is, in fact, exactly what many of these people are.

They make a living by selling you financial goods and services while acting as a disinterested giver of advice. All too often, they drown out the advisors who are working in their clients' best interests.

THERE IS NO SUCH THING AS
A FREE LUNCH—OR DINNER

Unfortunately, it's not that easy to meet an advisor working to the fiduciary standard. Why? They are often not the ones glad-handing, looking to meet clients.

Take the popular financial information lunches and dinners sponsored by those seeking to sell their financial 411. If you are over the age of fifty-five, you most certainly are familiar with this game. For the remaining youngsters, let us explain. All too often, those approaching retirement age receive solicitations inviting them to a complimentary meal at a local and well-regarded restaurant.

These events are ridiculously common—so much so that a few years ago AARP determined that if you were over the age of fifty-five, you had a one-in-ten chance of having attended one such event within the past three years. Just how bad are these seminars? Another study found that more than half the sales pitches reviewed by the surveyors contained exaggerations, false information, or other misleading statements. That doesn't count the 13 percent that could be described succinctly by the word "fraud."

The people who sell these products are good at what

they do. Their primary job is to sell their financial wares. They promise to solve our very real problems, and to address our entirely legitimate fears. Often, the first item in the playbook is to prey upon our mistrust of the government. Since writing and doing the reporting for *Pound Foolish,* Helaine has sat through many such meals over the years and has been repeatedly told that Social Security and Medicare are doomed—or at least bound to be drastically cut. Taxes are going to rise. She's in immediate danger of not being able to pay for her children's college. She will outlive her retirement savings. The solution? Whatever financial vehicle the broker making the presentation is pitching.

It's easy to assume that you would resist the hard sell. But it's possible you wouldn't. Under no condition should you attend these events. Helaine and Harold know no one who has been invited to a meal where simple budgeting strategies or low-cost index funds were discussed. Instead, the supposedly expert financial whiz leading the seminar is always selling a high-cost and often subpar-return product. Remember Harold's favorite phrase: "If it's free, you are the product." You might also consider his second-favorite saying: "If you sit down for cards, and you don't know who the sucker is—you do."

YOUR FINANCIAL ADVISOR IS NOT YOUR FRIEND

You've seen the ads. You've heard the promos. Merrill Lynch promises "trusted advice and innovative solutions for affluent individual investors." Banks like JPMorgan Chase say they establish strong personal relationships with their clients.

Well, yes, but . . .

The fact is many brokers are smart and nice. They'll commiserate with you about getting your ten-year-old to do his homework so you can worry about paying for Harvard. They understand that for many of us money is an intimate matter and that we hunger for sympathy and advice.

It doesn't matter. Your friendly neighborhood brokerage or bank is not a place to go for nonconflicted, fiduciary financial advice, any more than an appliance store is the best place to ask whether you really need a 3-D TV. A recent survey published by the *New York Times* proves the point. When Morningstar, the prominent investment research firm, reviewed the mutual funds offered by Goldman Sachs, Morgan Stanley, JPMorgan Chase, and Wells Fargo, it discovered a majority had underperformed their benchmarks for a decade.

Why do we fall for it? In many cases, you've been hearing the names of these brokerages and banks your entire life, and you consider them reliable and safe. But that's not the track record. For all too many of them, their customers are a lucrative revenue stream. Whether on salary or commission, frontline people and brokers are under intense pressure to meet sales quotas for various financial products. From "alternative investments" to "structured products" and simple mutual funds, most of what they have to offer will cost more, might well come with more risk than you realize, and will underperform a simple index fund.

Remember: Stock picking doesn't work. But your friendly neighborhood banker and broker have no obligation to share that information with you. Their business model (and often their self-image) rely on the belief that they are your friends and they can guide you through the financial maze, allowing you to triumph over—and often do better than—the markets.

It's a pretty good business model.

This is where Helaine likes to cite one of her favorite academic studies ever.

A group of professors hired a group of actors to play the role of consumers seeking financial advice. They gave the actors specially designed faux portfolios and sent them to a selection of leading brokerage houses and banks. The result?

Over and over again, would-be clients with perfect portfolios in well-diversified index funds were told to invest in high-fee investments, including managed mutual funds. People with imperfect portfolios were given imperfect advice; less than 10 percent of the brokers tested without their knowledge told their would-be clients to put their money in low-cost index funds. And just for an added kick, women were treated resoundingly worse than men and were more likely to receive financial advice from someone who didn't even bother to ask about their overall financial profile.

As if all this weren't depressing enough, almost none of the guinea pig clients had a clue about what had just happened. When the researchers asked them what they personally thought of the broker they had met with, 70 percent—yes, 70 percent!—said they were so impressed that they would consider returning with their own real-life investment portfolio in hand.

Lest you think this is only an American problem, a 2014 study examined the experience of Canadian consumers with financial advisors. On average, the advisors encouraged their customers to own more stock and earn about 1.7 percent higher annual returns. Unfortunately, the advisors charged a whopping 2.7 percent annual fee. This wiped out the advantages associated with stock ownership while leaving clients exposed to greater risk.

Take it from Melissa. She'd wisely put her funds in a low-cost group of index funds. But when her grandmother died and she received a small inheritance, she planned to move the money over to her main account. That is, until she spoke with her mom's financial advisor. He was friendly and sympathetic and promised to take care of everything. So she left him in charge of the newly acquired money.

Two years later, Melissa read an article about how fees can eat away at investments. Curious, she took a look at her own portfolios. Her original one was doing fine—low-cost index funds. But the one managed by the supposedly friendly broker? It had experienced significantly slower growth. When Melissa investigated, she discovered the fees were more than double those in her original portfolio. "I felt like such an idiot," she said. "I was taken in by a charismatic salesman."

IF YOU WANT GOOD ADVICE, PAY FOR IT

Do you work for free? Neither do financial advisors.

If you want unconflicted financial advice, you almost certainly have to pay for it.

Very few of us have any idea of how much we are paying for financial advice. According to a 2011 survey by Cerulli Associates, a market research firm, one-third of us thought we were receiving a free service when we turned to a broker for financial advice. Another third admitted to absolute befuddlement about how someone would be compensated for investment strategies.

This isn't because we are uniquely stupid. It's because it is not in the interests of almost anyone doling out financial advice for you to realize how much his counsel is going to cost—or that it is going to cost you anything at all.

Financial pitches are littered with promises of "free consultations" and "no charge for meeting." The financial advisors using them can get away with making these claims because they will indeed not get paid until they make a sale. Then all too many will receive a commission for pushing one financial product over another.

Helaine calls this the culture of commission. It can work a number of different ways. In one case, the financial advisor takes money right off the top. This is called a load, or a front-end fee. So let's say you are seeking to invest $100,000 in a fund with a (whopping but not atypical) 5 percent load. You'll pay $5,000 off the top for that investment.

There are also back-end loads. All of your money goes into the mutual fund or annuity, and the financial services company pays the broker his or her fee. Sounds like a bargain, right? Not exactly. In exchange, you agree to not move your money for several years or pay a substantial penalty for the privilege of doing so should the investment not work out or you change your mind.

Then there are trailing fees. That means the advisor selling the financial investment receives a commission for the sale for as long as you hold the investment. This is often around 0.5 percent, and it comes out of your investment year in and year out, regardless of whether it performs well or falls in value. If you stop to think about this, it obviously adds up.

Altogether, the Obama administration estimates that what it calls "backdoor payments and hidden fees" in the retirement savings industry are costing Americans up to $17 billion annually. And that's just for individual retirement accounts. Even the best, most well-intentioned broker is going to have a tremendous incentive to give you financial advice that will boost his own bottom line.

There are some fiduciaries who work on a commission basis. But that arrangement is uncommon. If someone is truly working to advance your financial best interests, why create an additional incentive to mess with your investments?

BEWARE THE FEE-BASED ADVISOR

Beware of the term "fee based." This is another one of the junk terms littering the financial advice industry. It means the advisor in question can charge a flat rate, but he or she might also work to commission. Some non-fiduciary brokers will also charge their clients for their advice, leaving the impression their advice is unbiased and meets the highest standards of care.

One way this works: The advisors charge a fee of up to several thousand dollars for sitting down with you and creating a formal financial plan. They then get to double dip, receiving commissions for the mutual funds, insurance, and other financial products they recommend you purchase as part of their plan. Unless you ask hard questions up front, you are unlikely to realize what's going on until you receive the formal advice—if at all.

Unfortunately, this is perfectly legal. There is only one way to avoid falling victim to a fee-based advisor. Never assume someone is a fiduciary. Never assume he doesn't ever work for commissions. Always ask.

You want to seek out an advisor who works on a fee-only basis. This means the advisor is paid by you—*and only by you*. That payment can take a number of forms:

Percentage of assets under management: This is an annual fee based on the amount of assets you are seeking advice on. The percent can range from as little as 0.15 percent for some of the online advisory services to 2 percent. (By the way, we think 2 percent is way too high a price to pay for financial advice.) Many advisors charge a sliding scale, with the percentage charged falling as the amount gets greater—for example, 1 percent charged for the first $500,000 and then 0.5 percent on the rest of the sum.

Flat fee: This is the financial advisor equivalent of a prix fixe meal. The financial advisor agrees to charge you one rate for a package of agreed-upon services. Perhaps that includes a budget review and overall financial plan. Or maybe it's a get-out-of-debt package.

Hourly rate: You sit down with a financial advisor. He starts a clock. You pay by the hour for the advice. This can cost as little as $50 an hour for a financial coach, the sort of person who doesn't make investment recommendations but can help you devise a budget and get-out-of-debt plan, to $250 to $500 an hour for someone with a certified financial planner credential.

If you're used to getting a service "for free," it's hard to pay real money for it. We understand that. But it was never free advice. You only thought it was a complimentary service. Not only didn't you know you were being charged, but you didn't know how much of a bill you were paying.

HOW DO YOU FIND A FIDUCIARY?

So what is a fiduciary?

These are credentials that indicate someone is almost certainly working to the fiduciary standard:

- certified financial planner (CFP)
- registered investment advisor (RIA)
- fee-only advisor

And how can you find one of these people? One way, of course, is to ask. Another is to call or e-mail some of the organizations that represent them. They include both accreditation organizations and certain financial planner networks that will only work to the fiduciary standard. They include the following:

- CFP: CFP Board, http://www.cfp.net
- fee-only advisor: National Association of Personal Financial Advisors (NAPFA), http://www.napfa.org

And how do you make certain someone is a fiduciary?
You need to ask and ask quite specifically: Do you work to the fiduciary standard at all times? This last part, "at all times," is important. As the fine print on brokerage forms indicates, the fact that an advisor commits to a fiduciary standard for some of her dealings with you does not hold her to this standard in others, even if she is providing detailed information and guidance. For example, even though CFPs are supposed to adhere to the fiduciary standard, there is a little loophole whereby they don't need to act as fiduciaries if

they are simply selling financial products and not offering planning services.

There is, unfortunately, no way around this question. If you ask someone if he is committed to offering advice in your best interests, a less-than-ethical financial salesperson could respond, "Would I ever not do that for you?" And you would be none the wiser.

Can these questions feel awkward? Sure. But again, if a financial advisor attempts to make you feel uncomfortable for asking, you should not be working with him or her.

Tara Siegel Bernard, a personal financial writer for the *New York Times,* recommends taking this even a step further. Never mind asking about the fiduciary standard. "Ask them to sign an oath stating they will act as fiduciaries," she writes. She suggests one put together by the advocacy group the Committee for the Fiduciary Standard.

Putting Your Interests First

I believe in placing your best interests first. Therefore, I am proud to commit to the following five fiduciary principles:

I will always put your best interests first.

I will act with prudence; that is, with the skill, care, diligence, and good judgment of a professional.

I will not mislead you, and I will provide conspicuous, full and fair disclosure of all important facts.

I will avoid conflicts of interest.

I will fully disclose and fairly manage, in your favor, any unavoidable conflicts.

ADVISOR FIRM   AFFILIATION DATE

Someone who is legally obliged to act in your best interests is almost certainly going to be happy to share that information with you. She'll likely welcome the question. It will make her look better to tell you that she is legally bound to put your interests ahead of her own. You and your family are trusting your advisor with a lot of money, maybe your life savings. You're entitled to ask her about her obligations to you.

CONSIDER USING ROBO-ADVISORS

Robo-advisors are the newest advisors on the block. Less than ten years old, these companies use computers in place of the human touch. Instead of sitting down with an advisor, would-be investors answer a series of questions about their financial history, goals, obligations, and risk tolerance. The algorithms then suggest a series of investments.

The fees for these companies vary, but they are significantly lower than those for traditional advisors. Robo-advisors have proven so popular that some mutual fund families and discount brokerages are starting their own. And no wonder. The advantage of the business model is obvious. Robo-advisors bring down the price of advice to something almost anyone can afford.

Not all online investment schemes are created equal, however. Some companies specialize in helping you select the right mix of low-cost index and exchange-traded funds, but other robo-advisors encourage you to trade individual stocks, options, and other stuff that should have no role in your life. Still others claim to offer the service for free but are making money in hidden fees.

No matter how good it sounds, you still need to ask if a robo-advisor is a fiduciary.

FIDUCIARY OR SUITABILITY, YOU STILL NEED
TO DO DUE DILIGENCE

Finally, we need to add a disclaimer. Seeing a fiduciary and paying for your own financial advice are no guarantees. You will still need to do due diligence. But you are more likely to be on firmer ground.

There are numerous places to look up your financial advisors' records, and, unfortunately, you might well need to check in more than one place. Check most brokers at the Financial Industry Regulatory Authority. If you are thinking of working with a certified financial planner, the CFP Board maintains disciplinary records on its members. State regulatory authorities also maintain databases. Our advice: Check them all.

You work hard for your money. Sometimes you will want advice on how to best handle it. Many of us can benefit from an objective, outside eye. The good news is—tough economic realities or not—you can still boost your own bottom line when you get aid. Just use the word "fiduciary." It just might change your financial life.

Rule #7:

Buy a Home When You Are Financially Ready

BUY A HOME FOR THE RIGHT REASONS

When Harold and Veronica moved from Ann Arbor to Chicago in 2003, they were excited to buy their first home. They were finally done writing rent checks, while their home-owning friends rode the escalator up the housing market.

There was only one problem. They were nowhere close to having the traditional 20 percent down payment. So Harold persuaded his new employer, the University of

Chicago, to provide a seven-year $50,000 second mortgage that he could use to purchase a new home. The recruitment deal specified that the university would make all the monthly payments—as long as Harold kept the job. When that $50,000 wasn't quite enough, Harold borrowed another $5,000 from his sister.

Eager to start house hunting, Harold called a university-recommended bank loan officer. That's when he got a blast of cold water. "You are not a good customer," the man bluntly explained. He noted that Harold would be in a bad position if his new job didn't work out or if the housing market went down instead of up.

Harold responded in the "Don't you know who I am?" fashion of the newly tenured academic. Then he went mortgage broker shopping. Because this was 2003, he found many happy to assist him. More than a decade later, his home worth about $70,000 less than what he paid for it, Harold realizes that the original loan officer offered him rare candor, not to mention excellent advice.

There is, unfortunately, no way to look into the future to see whether owning a home is the right financial move for you. But there are commonsense questions you can answer to determine if you are ready for the responsibility of home ownership.

OWNING A HOME IS NOT SOMETHING WE'VE ALWAYS DONE

Prior to the Great Depression, Americans were much more likely to be renters than homeowners. Why? Well, for starters, mortgages were limited. Home buyers needed to put up half the purchase price in cash, then pay off the remainder in five to ten years.

The Great Depression changed things. The sudden economic collapse meant that many couldn't pay off their loans. Foreclosures soared. Real estate prices plummeted. In an effort to stabilize the situation, the federal government introduced the 20 percent down mortgage that could be paid off over thirty years.

The newfangled concept got a huge boost after World War II, when low-rate, low-down-payment federally subsidized mortgages turned millions of returning veterans into homeowners. As the historians Glenn Altschuler and Stuart Blumin note, "Perhaps for the first time ever, a significant majority of American families had realized the dream of homeownership."

This system was far from perfect; there was rampant and codified racial discrimination, for starters. Yet for millions of new homeowners who benefited, this was a great achievement. They could live in a home and earn money on it at the same time. The downside? Those same millions began to view their homes as can't-miss investments.

HOME PRICES DON'T ALWAYS GO UP

Home prices can go up, or they can go down. Yet many people don't quite believe it. Even after the Great Recession's housing bust, Americans identify real estate as the best long-term investment. According to the February 2015 National Housing Survey, 46 percent of respondents believed home prices would rise over the next year. Only 6 percent believed that prices would fall.

For the majority of Americans, their home is their largest financial asset. The National Association of Home Builders claims a primary residence makes up 62 percent of a median homeowner's total assets. More Americans own a home than possess a retirement or brokerage account.

Owning a home is almost always what experts call a highly leveraged investment. That makes it a risky investment, even if it is hard to see risk in bricks. How does this work? Well, suppose you have a $200,000 home with a $180,000 mortgage on it. A 10 percent drop in your local housing market all but wipes out all of your home equity. If for some reason you can't make your monthly payments, you might lose the house you were counting on for your retirement, along with everything you invested in it.

HOME OWNERSHIP: AN EXPENSIVE AUTOMATIC SAVINGS PLAN?

In the best-case scenario, owning your own residence works as an automatic savings plan. You find a home. You put the traditional 20 percent cash down. You get a fixed-rate fifteen- or thirty-year mortgage, which you faithfully pay month after month. Once you have paid off your mortgage, you own a big asset. You never once thought you were putting money in a savings account or investing it. But that's exactly what you did.

This is the way many of our parents and grandparents bought a home. They had to save up for a 20 percent down payment (more about this in a minute). They then sat down with a banker who evaluated their finances. Only when that bank official said he was satisfied with their finances could they put the money down on the home of their dreams.

For millions of Americans, this system brought powerful advantages. Almost all mortgages were of the thirty-year fixed-rate variety. There were no adjustable rate mortgages that allowed you to only pay the interest for a period of time and then ballooned in payment to compensate.

It was also hard to buy more house than one could comfortably afford. If you couldn't or wouldn't document your income, you were out of luck; there was no such thing as the now infamous "no doc" loan. There were few options to put down less than 20 percent on a home. The bank officer would have laughed at the phrase "zero percent down." Certainly no one was lending you 100 or 110 percent of a property's value, as happened prior to the housing market crash.

Nor were your grandparents tempted to take a loan out against their home. What we call home equity lines of credit were then referred to as second mortgages, and they were difficult to obtain. You once again had to return to the bank and meet with a banker and explain both your financial need and your plans to pay the money back. If this doesn't sound too appetizing, that was the point. Putting your home equity "to work" playing the stock market, taking a "must-have" vacation to Fiji, or redoing the kitchen with the latest in Viking appliances occurred to almost no one.

If you followed this plan, your savings—tied up in your home—were in an impressively secure lockbox until you sold the property. This savings plan didn't rely on people's remembering to set money aside every month, invest it properly, and leave it alone. By paying down a mortgage, you did exactly that. This was the genius of the system.

That said, home ownership is an expensive savings plan. Sure, money is taken out of your account and invested every month in a way we expect will do well. But home ownership comes with an expense ratio that makes the most expensive mutual funds look like a bargain.

For starters, there are the mechanics of interest payments. In the first years of home ownership, the bank takes the vast majority of your monthly payment as interest, only crediting a small portion toward the principal on the loan. You can likely get some of that back as a credit on your taxes—provided, that is, if you itemize your return.

Then there are various property taxes. While a thirty-year fixed-rate mortgage will remain one fixed amount, taxes almost always increase over time. And you will need to pay that bill no matter what.

Finally, owning a home means maintaining it. Repairing leaky roofs and sinks, painting walls, planting gardens—there is always *something,* and that something costs money.

RENTING BRINGS RISK TOO

According to Nobel Prize–winning economist Robert Shiller, the S&P composite stock index has outperformed housing by roughly a factor of eight between 1890 and the end of 2014.

Not surprisingly, economists sometimes perform complex calculations to show that renting is sometimes a better overall deal than home ownership. Their advice? Calculate the difference in expenses, and invest the savings in a broad-based stock market index fund. You'll build more wealth in the long term, they say.

It's not bad advice. It is an especially valuable reminder that one should not deliberately spend more on a house than one needs in the hopes of a high financial return. But most of us have a way of spending the money one hoped to otherwise invest. Harold and Helaine believe about five people who are not economists or investment junkies have ever run this calculation and rigorously followed through on it. If you are one of those five, congratulations. Make sure to maximize your contributions to your 401(k) and other automatic savings to ensure that the money you hope to save goes straight where it belongs.

Moreover, renting long term comes with risks too. Rents can increase, sometimes dramatically. In many cities, including Los Angeles and San Francisco, rents have soared post-2008. If your salary does not keep up, you could eventually be priced out of a neighborhood where you've lived for many years and your children attend school. Currently, half of renters in the United States are paying more than the recommended 30 percent of income for their housing, leaving them on thin financial ice.

There is also something to be said for controlling your own environment. Landlords can decide they no longer want to be landlords, or at least no longer yours. It's also nice to paint the walls of your home a color of your choosing or simply live with a dog or cat if you wish without asking permission. There are, in other words, practical benefits to owning your own residence.

KNOW HOW MUCH HOME YOU CAN AFFORD

Experts recommend spending no more than a third of your take-home pay on housing. Any more than that, and your finances are going to be tight, leaving you financially vulnerable when something inevitably goes wrong. To be fair, this isn't always possible. In some places such as New York and San Francisco, it can be all but impossible.

One way to know exactly your home-buying budget is to get your mortgage preapproved by a bank before you look at the first house. Keep in mind, this isn't an exact science. Banks once overestimated what we could comfortably pay. Now in reaction to the real estate bubble, some underestimate it. Still, preapproval can give your housing budget a dose of reality.

Moreover, settling on a budget for your home is an essential first step. Unless you are a multimillionaire, you will face trade-offs. Decide what you want most before you go shopping. How many bedrooms must you have? Do you prefer an older home you can lovingly renovate over time, or do you prefer a just-built home that only requires you to unpack your boxes? Do you really need four bedrooms, or will three do just fine?

People in sales have a saying, "Buyers are liars," meaning that buyers might think they want one thing, but they really want another. It's a phrase that indicates contempt for the buyer. While you might believe you are shopping for the home of your dreams, to the real estate agent you are just another sale. Because real estate agents work on commission, they stand to make more money both by persuading you to buy a more expensive home than you intend and by minimizing the time spent with you.

It's easy to fall in love with a home. Many come with high-end designer appliances, gussied-up spa bathrooms, or other bells and whistles. But here is what you need to remember: The three most important things in a real estate purchase are location, location, and location. The creakiest home in a desirable neighborhood will likely do better for you—at least financially—over the long run than a gorgeous home in a lesser locale. Homes in highly rated school districts tend to hold more resale value and sell quicker when put on the market.

Many studies indicate that commutes matter too. An easy commute (or no commute) makes people much happier than that fancy kitchen upgrade. Really. A group of economists and psychologists surveyed more than nine hundred people about their satisfaction with various life chores and choices. The activity that made them the unhappiest: their morning commute.

Finally, don't fall prey to fears or real estate agents' insinuations that if you don't buy a home right now, you'll never get another chance. Try not to get too emotionally attached to any specific house either. There is always another home to buy. It's easier to drive a hard bargain when you are comfortable walking away. Harold and Veronica made the mistake of falling in love with their current house. By sorting out what you need and prioritizing what you want, you are less likely to make the same mistake.

HOMES ARE FOR THE LONG RUN

Home ownership, like stock investing, works best as a long-term proposition. It takes at least five years to have a reasonable chance of breaking even on a housing purchase. For the first few years, your mortgage payments mostly pay off the interest and not the principal. And there are many costs involved in moving in and selling a home. Unless you handle the sale yourself, you'll likely pay anywhere between 3 and 6 percent commission on a sale to a real estate agent.

20 PERCENT DOWN IS BEST

It's hard to save up to 20 percent of the purchase price of a home, especially if you live in a high-cost market. But the closer you can get to 20 percent, the better.

Why? The more money you can put down toward the initial purchase of a home, the lower your monthly mortgage payment. That's because you will need to borrow less money to finance the home. This can save you tens of thousands of dollars over the life of the loan. You'll probably get a lower interest rate too. The more you put down, the less likely you'll ever fall "underwater," with your home's market value dropping below what you still owe on your mortgage. Should you ever have an urgent need to sell, this is crucial.

If you put down less than 20 percent, you will need something called private mortgage insurance (PMI). The annual cost ranges from 0.5 percent to 1 percent of your home's value. That's more than $1,000 per year on a $200,000 home. You will need to pay that bill in addition to your monthly mortgage bill until the bank agrees that the combination of your rising home value and the amount you've paid down your mortgage principal leaves you owing less than 80 percent of the market value of your home. Why do you have to pay PMI? Because lenders believe that people who put less than 20 percent down on a property are more likely to default.

WHAT ABOUT A FIFTEEN-YEAR LOAN?

If you are looking to turbocharge your home equity, you might consider a fifteen-year loan instead of the conventional thirty-year loan. Fifteen-year loans come with a lower interest rate—usually by half a percent or so. The shorter lending period allows you to build up your nest egg faster, making for a better automatic savings plan. Harold has one of these.

Keep in mind, however, that despite the lower interest rate, fifteen-year mortgages require higher monthly payments because you are paying your loan off in half the time. If you don't have much of an emergency fund and you struggle with credit cards, student loans, or your monthly cash flow, a fifteen-year mortgage is not for you.

PLAIN-VANILLA FIXED RATE IS BEST

If you have good reason to believe you won't own the home for more than five or ten years, or if interest rates stay quite low, an adjustable rate mortgage (ARM)—that is, a mortgage that begins with a lower interest rate but can increase after a set period of time—might sound appealing. The same is true for interest-only loans, which are sometimes available to people with high income and net worth.

Suppose again that you are shopping for a $200,000 mortgage. You get on the Web and check out interest rates for competing products. On the particular day we looked, we saw the following:

Type of mortgage	Interest rate	Approximate monthly payment (from Internet mortgage calculator)
Thirty-year fixed rate	3.82%	$934
Fifteen-year fixed rate	3.05%	$1,386
5/1 adjustable rate	3.19%	$864 (initial payments)
Interest-only rate	4%	$666 (initial payments)

True, you can lower your initial monthly payments by getting an ARM or interest-only loan. Compared with a conventional thirty-year mortgage, the ARM saves you about $70 per month over the first five years of the loan. But there's a real risk. If interest rates rise, your monthly payment can really rise too.

At this writing, interest rates are near historic lows. There is a serious risk that your ARM will eventually cost more, maybe much more. Why bring more complexity and uncertainty into your life? You could get hit with a significant bill if your plans or circumstances change or the economy doesn't perform as you expect.

We like what Elizabeth Warren calls the "plain-vanilla" options: the traditional fifteen- or thirty-year fixed-payment mortgage, preferably with 20 percent down. If you can't afford that, chances are your budget is stretched in other ways too. You don't want to make yourself more vulnerable to a financial setback.

YOUR EMERGENCY SAVINGS ACCOUNT COMES FIRST

We know how much you want that home. And you have the down payment in hand. But . . . we need to ask, "Do you have a fully funded emergency savings account?" If you don't, do not pass go. Stop reading this chapter, go back and read chapter 1, and don't come back until you have a cash stash. And no, your emergency fund is absolutely not your down payment.

Helaine and Harold have owned homes for more than two decades between the two of them. We've learned that, well, stuff happens.

Helaine experienced a heater ignition that went dead during a cold snap, not to mention a basement that needed extensive drainage. In one never-to-be-forgotten week, her dishwasher suddenly died, followed a few days later by the equally sudden failure of her apparently bereaved refrigerator; they had shared the same kitchen for many years. Harold had a blown furnace, a basement water leak, eight windows that needed to be replaced, and a raccoon who ate his way into the attic.

Our lives don't cooperate either. We all receive unexpected financial setbacks. Someone gets sick. The insurance company denies a medical claim. A job is suddenly lost. However life intrudes, the bank still expects to receive our monthly mortgage payments.

Neither our houses nor our lives are fixed. Be prepared.

Finance your emergency fund. *Then* think about purchasing a home. If you don't have an emergency fund and do own a house, chances are good you will someday find yourself in financial turmoil.

GET YOUR DEBT UNDER CONTROL
BEFORE HOME BUYING

When you apply for a mortgage, the bank or mortgage broker will ask you about your monthly debt obligations. That includes credit card debt, student loans, car loans, and any other real estate obligations. If the combination of that debt with the amount you want to borrow exceeds 43 percent of your income, you will have a hard time getting a mortgage. Your "debt-to-income ratio" will be deemed too high, and mortgage issuers—not to mention the federal government—will consider you at high risk for a future default.

In this situation, it will be hard to find a bank to issue you a conventional mortgage. It's possible you will find someone to issue you what is called a nonconforming loan; that is, a mortgage that does not meet government criteria. It won't be insured by the federal government, and it will carry a higher interest rate. Banks are not crazy and mean for insisting on these sorts of guidelines. If your debt is high, home owner-ship is going to be a stretch, and you're more likely to fall into financial distress if something goes wrong.

SHOP FOR A MORTGAGE

According to the Consumer Financial Protection Bureau, almost half of us do not shop for a mortgage when we begin the process of shopping for a home. We get it. Shopping for one mortgage is intimidating enough.

Comparison shopping is essential. Bank officers and mortgage brokers often have an interest in steering you toward one particular mortgage. They don't have a fiduciary duty to exclusively pursue your own financial interests. They can steer you into a higher-interest mortgage or one with more fees and closing costs attached simply because it enhances their own or their company's bottom line.

This can really cost you. And unlike that overpriced $5 latte, you'll be stuck paying for an overpriced mortgage for years, maybe decades. The difference between a $200,000 mortgage offered at 4 percent and one offered at 4.5 percent comes to about $700 a year. That's about $21,000 over the life of a thirty-year mortgage. That's too much to give away.

So shop around. Call more than one bank or mortgage broker. Look at online mortgage comparison and informational sites, such as Bankrate.com and the CFPB's Know Before You Owe.

RESEARCH REFINANCING OPTIONS

Suppose you already have a mortgage and are living in your home. When should you refinance to take advantage of lower interest rates? The answer isn't obvious, because you have to pay for a title search, property appraisal, and more. You can generally expect to pay up front at least 2 percent of the value of your mortgage before you are done. Refinancing is rarely worth the hassle if your interest rate drops by less than one percentage point or if you're planning to move soon. Web calculators can help you weigh the benefits and costs, which depend on your tax rate, how much you owe, and how long you plan to stay in your present home.

It's easier to refinance if your mortgage obligations are less than 80 percent of the appraised value of your home. That's not always a firm requirement. If you've been keeping up on your payments but the value of your home has

declined, you may still be able to refinance at a lower interest rate through the government's Home Affordable Refinance Program.

FLIP PANCAKES, NOT HOUSES

"MAKE MONEY FROM INCOME PROPERTIES," read a
recent piece of mail Helaine received. "Wouldn't you like to
change the financial course for you and your family?"

There's a world of seminars and books out there promis-
ing you can buy real estate on the cheap, fix it up, and either
flip it for a quick profit or rent it out, making a decent
monthly income in the process.

Don't go there. Your house is your home. It is not a
speculative investment. Real estate speculation is best
reserved for gamblers and the pros.

Handling rental properties is an actual job that requires
specific expertise. Professional property managers have
ample financial reserves to weather a down market or times
when tenants can't pay their rent. They have the skills, time,
or money to replace damaged water heaters or faulty wiring.
They can research local markets. They're the people who

recently took a pass on that tempting investment property you're now considering.

If that isn't you, don't dabble. Just step away.

HOME BUYING—A CHECKLIST

We want you to buy a home if you think it is right for you. Harold owns the house he lives in, and Helaine loves her co-op. If you follow the basic rules below, it can be a smart financial decision:

- Get your debt under control, and save up your emergency fund.

- Save up as close to a 20 percent down payment as you can.

- Shop around (and get preapproved) for a fifteen- or thirty-year fixed-rate mortgage.

- Consider what you really want and need in a home, and stay consistent with your budget.

- Location, location, location.

- Enjoy your new home.

Rule #8:
Insurance—Make Sure You're Protected

WHEN BAD THINGS HAPPEN TO INSURED PEOPLE

Life was good for Bob and Jean. They had a nice house in the suburbs of a big city. Bob was a corporate executive with a Fortune 500 company. It was a good living, but he traveled a lot. As a result, Jean had spent a few years as a stay-at-home mom with their two children. She had recently returned to work as a teacher's aide. They had money set aside for emergencies, retirement, and the children's college. All was good. Life was on track.

And then Bob woke up with a headache one day. He took two aspirin and left for work. A few hours later, Jean received an emergency phone call. Bob had collapsed at the office.

Bob survived, but he could no longer work. Jean couldn't work for several months, and even when she did return to her job, it wasn't as if she could replace his income.

Mercifully, Bob had disability insurance. It couldn't replace his entire income—not even close. But it kept the family from falling into the financial abyss while he was suffering from a medical crisis and gave them the breathing room to recalibrate their lives.

Let's face it, nobody wants to deal with insurance, for the same reason that we don't want to spend our spare time trying to figure out what disaster will befall us. It's depressing. It's scary. It's . . . absolutely essential if you plan on taking control and protecting your finances.

Insurance is a complicated but necessary evil. Few people have enough cash lying around to cover a lengthy hospital stay, loss of a home, loss of a loved one, or loss of income from a family member's illness. In exchange for a monthly premium, insurance can protect us from the financial fallout of tragedy. Going without proper insurance could destroy all the hard work you did in the previous parts of this book.

As always, where there is fear and there are commission-based salespeople, there will be people looking to exploit and profit from that fear. In this chapter, we hope to arm you with just enough information for you to get the best insurance for your needs.

LIFE INSURANCE

What would happen to your family and loved ones if something suddenly were to happen to you? Would your spouse be okay? Your children? Or maybe your elderly parents are counting on you to help them out in their old age. When money is tight or you're healthy, it's easier (and a lot less stressful) to not think about these kinds of questions. Yet if something goes wrong, not being prepared for it will truly be the biggest financial blunder you'll ever make.

Life insurance is insurance that pays off when the person covered by the policy dies.

Most people think about life insurance as replacing the wages of the primary earner, but many stay-at-home parents should also consider purchasing coverage. The annual

Mom Salary Survey estimates that a mom (yes, we know, it could be a dad too) often provides services worth more than $100,000 a year if you actually needed to purchase these services, instead of relying on love, for their delivery.

Where to start? Simply calling, e-mailing, or texting a life insurance company that comes up online or solicits you is not always the best approach. Why? Life insurance is almost always sold on a commission basis. The types of insurance that pay salespeople the highest commissions are the ones you need the least.

The best type of insurance to protect your loved ones, at the least cost to your pocketbook, is called term insurance.

Term insurance offers protection for a set period of time—usually anywhere between one and thirty years. You pay an annual fee, and you are covered for another year. It's sort of like paying rent, but instead of getting a two-bedroom apartment with a balcony, you get peace of mind and the ability to sleep at night.

Term policies also come with various add-ons that can increase the cost of the policy. We recommend a policy that keeps the price of the insurance the same amount every year for the period of time covered by the policy. This is called level term. Why? Without the level term guarantee, the cost of your annual premium can suddenly surge.

Our advice: Get a thirty-year level term life policy, even if you are not convinced you will need the policy for that long. Why? Because if you guess wrong, there is no guarantee you will be able to get another life insurance policy or a policy at a price you can afford. And of course, you can simply cancel the policy after twenty years if you decide you no longer need it. It's a rental after all. You can move on at any time.

And make sure to go bargain hunting when you are looking for insurance. Don't go to your cousin's son or your best friend's daughter, because he or she seems like a nice person. Talk to a few different agents. Go online, and check out quotes from comparison-shopping sites like Insure.com.

Moreover, stay alert. Many insurance sales professionals won't recommend term life insurance. Instead, they will try to talk you into something called whole life or universal life insurance, also known as a cash value policy. These policies offer you life insurance protection while also allowing you to invest the money in the stock market. Insurance agents often pitch it as a policy that allows you to sleep at night while making your money grow. Why would you want to throw your money away on a policy you are renting, like term life insurance? Own the policy, enjoy the benefit of investing, and you'll get something for your money.

These salespeople might also try to sell you on whole or universal life insurance by saying it will cover your estate taxes after you die. If someone says this to you, chances are you need to find a new broker. Only about two out of every thousand estates are subject to federal estate taxes. Married couples need to amass and leave an estate of $10.86 million before the federal tax man comes calling upon their death.

Another sales pitch: a way to outsmart college financial aid offices. You will be told you can invest money in a life insurance policy and colleges will not count the sum as part of your assets when determining your need. That is a huge red flag for any investment.

What the eager sellers of these policies won't say: This stuff pays much higher commissions than term life insurance. That's why they prefer it to term insurance.

In fact, you can think of whole life insurance as a ridiculously overpriced automatic investment scheme. It costs more than term insurance, and not by a small amount. Think multiples. (Someone has to pay the commission, after all!) Plus, it's not as if you can invest this money in the lowest-cost index fund you can find. The investment options are limited and selected by the insurer, and you can be sure that they are not going to be the lowest-cost index funds available. They are often high-fee options.

Oh, and as for the college savings component? The financial aid offices at private, independent colleges are onto it, so good luck with that.

And don't just rely on the life insurance you receive through your job. If you are offered insurance as a benefit through work, it's likely you'll receive a small but decent amount—usually around one or two years of your salary. It's a nice backup, especially because you are not paying for it. But you need to think of it as a backup, not your primary coverage. It certainly won't remain free—if you are even eligible to take it all—if you leave the job, and there is no guarantee you'll be offered a competitive rate if you can keep it.

One last point that should be obvious: The younger and healthier you are, the cheaper your life insurance bill will be.

SOCIAL SECURITY DISABILITY ISN'T ENOUGH

Many people can obtain disability insurance through their employer. If you are one of these people, run, don't walk, and sign up now. No one plans to become so disabled that they cannot work. But it happens, and it happens more often than you realize. According to the Council for Disability Awareness, one in four twenty-year-olds will become disabled before they reach retirement age. And no, Social Security Disability Insurance payments, known familiarly as SSDI, are not a path to riches and a life of ease. The average monthly payment is rather low, currently about less than $1,200 a month, much lower than private disability insurance. Nor is the sign-up process for SSDI automatic. While a minority of application claims are approved in as little as a month, many others can take several years—if they are accepted at all, that is. The majority of applications are ultimately denied. There is also an additional waiting period for the accompanying medical coverage.

Once again, you've worked hard to secure your financial foundation. Sad things do happen. One of Harold's friends recently had a serious stroke in his early fifties.

Don't let a debilitating illness be the crack that undermines the hope of a secure future.

PLAYING THE INSURANCE TRIFECTA—RENTAL, HOMEOWNER, AND AUTO

The goal of this sort of insurance is not to pick up the cost of every single repair bill or thing gone wrong, from a broken window to a lost six-year-old computer. It is to *protect your net worth.*

Homes are all too often the largest asset most American families possess. As a result, when it comes to homeowner's coverage, keep your eye on the prize. Many insurance companies have a less-than-stellar track record when it comes to stepping up to the plate during catastrophes. Forget the heartwarming commercials proclaiming their overwhelming loyalty to you in your time of need, complete with goofy guardian angels and their Tina Fey–like banter.

Turn to the news instead, where you can find tales of insurance adjusters lowballing homeowners who have suffered hurricane or flood damage during Hurricane Sandy or altogether denying their claims based on technicalities.

How can you prevent denials? Understand exactly what kind of coverage is contained in the policy you are buying. You need to pose worst-case scenarios to the person selling the policy and then make sure to get their answers in writing. For instance, if you live near water, get flood insurance. Make sure your flood insurance covers you against rising waters, not just burst pipes. Double-check how they define flood coverage. For instance, if a hurricane-like wind busts your living room window and rain and hurricane waters surge into your home, are you covered? That's likely to be considered wind damage, not flood damage. Make sure your homeowner's policy covers that.

Here's one pro tip: Go for the high-deductible options. You won't be using this insurance very often unless you are a fantastically unlucky person. Harold, for instance, has never used his homeowner's policy, not even once. Why? Because when it comes to minor repairs—like a broken window—he pays for it with his emergency fund. Unlike, say, catastrophic events, like the time his stepsister's house was hit by lightning and burned to the ground. Fortunately, she was covered.

Needless to say, the higher the deductible—that is, the

amount of money you need to spend before insurance begins to kick in—the lower your annual tab. *But that's a bad deal!* We can hear you saying, "I mean, what if I have $2,000 worth of damage, and a $1,000 deductible? I'll be out $1,000 plus whatever co-payment I am responsible for." Well, yes. But how often do you plan to file $2,000 claims?

High-deductible insurance is cheaper for a more subtle reason too. People who buy such plans don't expect to file many claims. That's reflected in the monthly premiums.

How much you will save with a high-deductible plan depends on the specifics, but the savings can be substantial. And this is true of all insurance, not just homeowner's. According to one survey commissioned by Insurance Quotes.com, car owners can save approximately 9 percent by raising their auto insurance deductible from $500 to $1,000 and 15 percent by raising it from $500 to $2,000. So examine your options.

On that note . . . car insurance.

No, you don't need it for the day you are almost but not quite sideswiped on Pacific Coast Highway while driving your children to day camp, as recently happened to Helaine and her husband. (It cost $300 to replace the sheared-off side-view mirror—an experience they got to relive for several days because no one came to clear the mirror from the side of the road.)

You probably do need coverage for what happened to Harold and Veronica while we were writing this chapter. Their 2004 Toyota Sienna was totaled when Veronica was rear-ended at a red light by a careless driver.

The point of auto coverage is twofold: You want to protect against collision and liability. Collision protects your car, which is why you will often hear people say you can live without it if you drive an older car. An insurer will cover only the book value of the auto, not what it would actually cost you to replace it or what you happen to think your car is worth. The cheapest 2015 Toyota Sienna carries a manufacturer's suggested retail price of about $28,600. How much did the insurance company pay Harold and Veronica for their totaled minivan? Three thousand four hundred sixty-nine dollars.

Liability is the important part and what you need to pay the most attention to. Whatever you do, do not sign up for the minimum coverage. Why? Once again, this is what insurance is for. Liability pays the bills if you are in an accident, and someone—and that means anyone in the accident—is injured. If it's a bad one and you don't have adequate liability insurance, financial life as you know it will be over. You could be forced to sell a home to cover the bills, or see your salary garnisheed, which is a fancy legal way of saying a portion of your salary will be taken out automatically, not for your benefit, but for the benefit of someone else.

So what is adequate liability insurance? It's at least twice the amount—and maybe more—of your net worth. Because liability coverage is not endless, it is recommended that people with a high net worth, or high salary, or people who believe their salary or assets will be significantly higher in the future, get something called umbrella insurance. Umbrella insurance covers the amount of your potential responsibility should you exhaust your liability insurance, just as an umbrella protects you on a rainy day. The metaphors in the insurance biz are not exactly subtle.

Finally, rental insurance. Rental insurance protects your possessions if you live in a rented home as well as offers you liability coverage, the same way homeowner's insurance does. Because it does not need to actually cover the residence itself—the landlord's homeowner's insurance does that—it's quite inexpensive. You may be tempted to skip the renter's insurance, which, after all, usually isn't required, but we would beg you not to. First, all the things that can happen to a home can also happen to your possessions, and you would like to replace them in the case of a fire or other catastrophe. A quick note: Rental insurance will allow you to choose between replacement cost and the actual cash value of your possessions. Replacement cost should cover the cost of buying your possessions new (yes, sometimes there are disputes about this). Actual cash value means what your actual goods are worth at the moment they needed to be replaced. What's the difference? If you need a new couch, replacement costs should cover a new one of similar quality to the old one. The actual cash value could leave you scrolling through Craigslist.

Second, liability—that word again. If your dog bites the Chinese food deliveryman or the next-door neighbor's child, no one cares if you rent or own. You can still get sued.

HEALTH INSURANCE

Here's the good news. No matter what you think of the Affordable Care Act (ACA)—a.k.a. ObamaCare—everyone can now get health insurance. No one can turn you down for a preexisting condition or decide retroactively you had a preexisting condition that you did not disclose. This is an amazing thing.

But as with other forms of insurance, you still need to be an educated consumer. There is no substitute for directly investigating the options open to you.

If you lack access to insurance through your employer, you can either sign up through a state health insurance marketplace or obtain it privately. If your income is below certain minimums, you may receive financial help for marketplace-based insurance. You can start shopping at the website, HealthCare.gov. The Kaiser Family Foundation has a fantastic, somewhat-less-forbidding webpage, "Understanding Health Insurance" (http://kff.org/understanding-health-insurance/), that answers frequently asked questions and lets you know what is available in your area.

Exchange plans come in four varieties—bronze, silver, gold, and platinum. The bronze plans have high out-of-pocket limits for in-network services of $6,000; the others—silver, gold, and platinum—have lower deductibles but progressively higher premiums. As they say, it's a trade-off. As the Kaiser website explains, the silver plan offers key advantages for many people.

As for your subsidies, they depend on your calendar-year income. If you had previously underestimated your income, and thus received a larger subsidy during the year than you were entitled to, you will need to pay money back to the government at tax time. On the other hand, you will get money back if you overestimated what you would earn.

Moreover, no plan—whether offered through an employer or purchased on the exchanges—guarantees that you are fully protected. According to the management consultancy Aon Hewitt, the amount of money people who receive plans through their employers are expected to pay in premiums and for out-of-pocket expenses has grown by more than 50 percent since 2010. Why? The cost of co-pays and deductibles has soared. Moreover, there is no rule saying that out-of-network charges be counted toward either the deductible or your out-of-pocket maximum payment. If you sign up for a health maintenance organization (HMO) or exclusive provider organization (EPO), they generally won't be.

If this seems ridiculously complicated—not to mention budget busting—well, you are right. The sad fact is that health-related debt is one of the leading causes of bankruptcy, and the majority of those people who had to declare bankruptcy had health insurance when they were ill. The problem wasn't that they lacked health insurance. Their financial woes were caused by all the things the health insurance company would not cover and the bills that piled up because they or a loved one could not work.

These are serious problems. But none of them provide good reason for you to go without health insurance. Nor is the fact that health insurance can be very expensive and you are in fine health a reason to do without it. Nothing—and we mean nothing—can send you into bankruptcy faster than the lack of health coverage.

So how can you best protect yourself financially in this climate?

- Comparison shop every year for your health insurance, even if the government heavily subsidizes your coverage. This year's most economical choice might not remain a good deal in later years.

- Do your homework to ensure that your plan includes the doctors and hospitals most important to you. If a plan claims to include your doctor, double-check that with the doctor's office. Also double-check hospital coverage. You don't want to discover after you or a loved one becomes ill that a nearby hospital or specialty center is not covered by your plan.

- Maintain a strong emergency fund. You can still face large out-of-pocket costs if you get sick. These often amount to thousands of dollars if you need costly medications or services.

A final note: Some people believe that the Affordable Care Act allows you to "go bare" and then to run out and buy insurance if you get sick or injured. That's not how it works. You can buy marketplace coverage only during specific enrollment periods or when you experience what is referred to in exchange-speak as "a qualifying life event," such as divorce or job loss or a move to a new state. If you have a stroke or get hit by a car at any other time of the year, you're in trouble.

CONSIDER PROTECTING YOUR RETIREMENT

As we discussed earlier in the book, there is much concern about our paltry retirement savings and how to make it last. Don't think the insurance industry isn't onto it. It has many fancy life insurance products that are marketed as making it nearly impossible to run out of money after you stop working.

Only two are worth considering.

The first is something called an immediate annuity. That's an insurance product that when you sign up, you turn over a sum of money and, in return, receive a set monthly payment for life. The strength of an immediate annuity is its simplicity. It will indeed pay you a set amount of money for your lifetime. The downside is the low payout provided at current interest rates. Right now, a sixty-five-year-old man seeking an immediate fixed annuity will turn over $100,000 to receive about $550 a month—this amount will not rise with inflation. A woman, because she's expected to live longer, will receive less.

Not surprisingly, many are leery of turning over the funds for such a small return. As a result, more attention is being paid to something called a longevity annuity, which is a fancy semi-new name for a deferred annuity. That's an annuity in which you turn over money now and then receive payment at a future date; many recommend age eighty or eighty-five. This ensures you won't outlive your money, no matter how old you are. You can even pay extra to obtain inflation protection. The plus side of a longevity annuity is that you will pay a lot less money up front than you will for an immediate annuity for this guarantee. The downside is the reason why:

The issuer is gambling that many who purchase a longevity annuity won't live to collect, or collect much. (Yes, some insurers will include a benefit that your heirs can get your principal back. But they charge extra for that.)

Our advice: We think longevity annuities are a great idea, provided it is a fixed annuity. If you decide to go this route, make sure you are getting a low-cost annuity. The best way to do this is to turn to a low-cost provider like Vanguard or TIAA-CREF.

And you do need to be careful. Once again, where there are insurance agents working on commission, there are people who will lead you astray. This is particularly prevalent when it comes to annuities, because there are so many confusing variations, all carrying the same name. What you want to avoid are variable annuities and equity annuities, which are also called indexed annuities. These are high-expense policies that allow for stock market investment, with some guarantee of a stop on losses. They sound great. Unfortunately, the fees are so high and the potential gains so capped you will almost always be better off investing on your own. So why are they pushed? Well, commissions are high—sometimes higher than 10 percent. You don't need to be giving your money away.

UNNECESSARY INSURANCE; OR, WHEN YOU DON'T NEED AN UMBRELLA FOR A SUNNY DAY

Here is a way to save money in the future. Some people sell insurance that can sound really tempting but that you don't need. We're talking about the fast-talking salesman who persuades you to buy insurance for the new refrigerator, or the credit card company that tries to sell you a policy to pay off your credit card bill if you are fired from your job. Most car insurance policies cover rental cars, so you probably don't need to pay for that when you rent a car. Identity theft insurance is also not very helpful. And no one—and we mean no one—needs a life insurance policy on a newborn baby. Yes, we're looking at you, Gerber.

There is, in our view, only one exception to this rule. If you have teenage children, make sure to take the offered insurance on their cell phones. Just trust us on this one.

PROTECT YOURSELF AGAINST BAD PROTECTORS

Even if you buy a great-sounding insurance policy, there's no guarantee that your insurer will come through for you when something bad happens. Buy insurance from a reputable company that you've heard of—one that scores well in buying guides such as *Consumer Reports*. You don't want to discover that your insurer is crummy while dealing with an awful event. Of course there are no guarantees.

As you probably heard nine million times in the ObamaCare debate, health insurers sometimes don't cover widely accepted cancer therapies. Others wrongly deny claims or drag their feet in covering something important. Your auto insurer may deny your claim on the basis that your car isn't worth repairing. Your homeowner's insurance might nickel-and-dime you over the replacement value of your stuff. In the aftermath of Hurricane Sandy, prominent flood insurers and engineering firms are alleged to have fraudulently modified damage assessment reports to understate storm damage.

You have legal options if this happens to you. In the case of health insurance, ACA requires health plans to establish a fair claims appeal and review process to resolve such disputes. If this process proves ineffective, your next sensible stop would be to contact your state insurance commission or department of insurance, which typically has jurisdiction over such matters. That's also your first call for any dispute involving your auto, rental, or homeowner's insurance. Staff there can indicate your specific options.

If you believe that your insurer has been dishonest or fraudulent, you can go to DEFCON 2 by contacting your state attorney general. That has an amazing way of getting your insurer's attention when all other efforts have failed.

THE SIX GOLDEN RULES OF INSURANCE

- When it comes to life insurance, stick with term.

- When it comes to property insurance, the higher the deductible the better.

- Always double-check that your hospital and doctor are on your health insurance plan.

- Adequate liability coverage is at least twice your net worth.

- Avoid complicated annuities.

- Keep an emergency fund.

Rule #9:

Do What You Can to Support
the Social Safety Net

WHAT YOU'VE LEARNED—AND EARNED—SO FAR

By following the easy-to-understand rules on our index card, you've likely made important and lasting changes to your financial life.

You have a better idea of how much money is coming in every week and month and how much is going out.

You've likely thought about what you want to accomplish with your financial life and made cutbacks in certain areas so that you can get there.

Your financial foundation is firmer, allowing you to rest easier.

You have an emergency savings fund, which allows you to meet unexpected expenses without resorting to expensive credit cards to get by when the car breaks down or the supermarket bill is larger than expected.

You are saving more money for everything from next summer's vacation to retirement.

You are getting more bang for your buck.

You are no longer falling prey to the get-rich-quick schemes of shady financial brokers, who view their first duty their own bottom line, not yours.

You've found a financial advisor with a fiduciary duty to you, and you are now invested in a group of low-cost index funds.

You are spending less time thinking of, worrying about, and handling your money than you did in the past. Budgeting software makes it easy to keep track of your spending. Automatic savings allows for withdrawals to be made to everything from emergency savings accounts to retirement savings accounts without lifting a finger.

Placing the money in index funds allows you to give little thought to your investments.

An insurance revamp is allowing you—hopefully—to spend less money on it, even as you have better protection.

You are now enjoying your life, getting more of what you want. You are moving forward.

That's why we wrote this book.

But we need to be honest: Budgeting, saving, low-cost investing, and otherwise doing the right financial thing can't protect us from everything. Because sometimes . . .

WE ALL NEED A LITTLE HELP

This is hard to admit. Most of us have some idea that there is a personal finance magic bullet. There is something we can do, something we can invest in, and, voilà, we'll be protected from all bad luck, and we will never need to worry about money again.

It would be lovely if it were true. But unfortunately, it's not.

Harold's life exemplifies both sides of the equation. He's been a diligent saver, has made good financial decisions (over the past decade, anyway), and is on a path to financial security.

Yet much of Harold's financial success relies on the

simple fact that he has a stable job with a great salary and generous benefits. He also has tenure, which means he basically can't be fired, something that very few other Americans can say.

But even with all that, Harold's story would certainly have played out differently without serious help from the American taxpayer. When he and his wife assumed the responsibility for his brother-in-law Vincent, they needed to turn to Medicare, Medicaid, Social Security, and other supports for people with intellectual disabilities like subsidized group housing. If these things didn't exist, Harold's family would likely have gone through all their accumulated resources, and then some.

It can unfold differently—and almost certainly would have a mere few decades earlier. Helaine's husband's grandmother was diagnosed with cancer in the early 1960s. The family pursued every treatment possible to save her. It didn't matter. She died—and left her son so broke that when Helaine's husband was born a few months after his grandmother's death, his parents had less than $600 to their name. This was, as you can guess, before the adoption of Medicare.

Yet all too often we do not want to admit to our need.

According to Suzanne Mettler, a professor of government at Cornell University, 96 percent of us have, at some point in our lives, turned to government financial supports to either get by or improve our own personal financial situation. When Mettler ran surveys asking people who had taken advantage of various government subsidies or benefits, she discovered a nation of people in denial.

More than 40 percent of people who have received Social Security, unemployment insurance, or a student loan did not appear to realize the source of the largesse. When asked, they denied they had ever used a government social program.

THE GOVERNMENT—YOUR LAST-RESORT INSURANCE

Let's be clear: Social Security is a government program. So is Medicare. Student loans come from the government, as does unemployment insurance. When you take a mortgage deduction on your income taxes, that's also a result of federal government largesse.

Almost all of us have, at some point in our lives, relied on the government for services so we can get by or make our situations better.

The truth is that our financial lives as we know them would be much harder and more precarious without the benefit of government social programs. All our financial planning and good financial behavior could be undone by one or two pieces of bad financial luck.

Both Harold and Helaine know plenty of friends and relatives who are every bit as financially disciplined as Harold yet who are having a much harder time because they have more modest incomes or because someone lost a job, got sick or injured, or otherwise experienced bad financial luck. Many people are really strapped.

Without Social Security, almost half of elderly Americans would probably live in poverty. It's the largest pension and protection most of us will ever see. Among elderly beneficiaries, just over half of married couples and almost three-quarters of those who are single receive at least 50 percent of their annual income from Social Security. There is no substitute for it.

Why are we telling you this? It is important to show our support for programs like Social Security and Medicare so that you can turn to the insurance backer of last resort, the government, if things go wrong. Without these programs, financial life as we know it would be harsher, harder, and likely not possible. We would be subject to sudden income shocks with absolutely no cushion to speak of. They are our first and last insurer. They allow us to sleep easily at night and enjoy our lives as much as all the other planning you've done.

So how can you do this? Speak up. When someone decries Social Security as a Ponzi scheme, remind him or her that many elderly would lead much poorer lives without it. When you hear someone say the government should keep its mitts off Medicare, speak up and say it is a government program.

But it's more than that. We need to admit we are the 96 percent. Be honest about not just what you pay in taxes but what you receive in return. Almost all of us have been helped—or have friends or relatives who have been helped—by unemployment insurance, Medicaid, food stamps, Pell Grants to attend college, or other government offerings. All too often, we take them for granted, but without them many of us would be in worse financial shape. Acting together, we can protect one another against financial and health risks that would crush any one of us, were we forced to face them unassisted.

We must take care of ourselves and our immediate

families through better planning, saving, and investing. When we do that, we are in a better place. But we must take care of our fellow citizens too. That's the best way to ensure that all the new changes we've adopted over the course of this book have the best chance for success.

Rule #10:

Remember the Index Card

This is where our book ends. But you are just getting started.

So remember, you don't need to be a financial whiz to understand and act on all the things we've discussed in these pages.

This is not rocket science. If it were, it wouldn't all fit so neatly on one four-by-six-inch index card.

With the card, it never has to be hard.

Hang it up on your fridge.

Take a screenshot of it so you can keep it on your phone.

Carry it around in your pocket.

Make it the default screen saver on your laptop.

Heck, have it tattooed on your arm if you want.

The only defense against the onslaught of information and the warp speed at which we're expected to process it is still good old-fashioned simplicity and common sense.

When in doubt, the index card is there to remind you of that.

Now stop worrying about your financial life, and enjoy your life!

Helaine and Harold

ACKNOWLEDGMENTS

Acknowledgments begin with the people who helped put the book together. So we would jointly like to thank our agent, Andrew Stuart, for his early enthusiasm for this project. At Portfolio, Adrian Zackheim, Tara Gilbride, Jackie Burke and Leah Trouwborst are terrific people to have in your corner, as is Niki Papadopoulos, who is the most extraordinary of editors. Elizabeth Shreve is both an excellent publicist and wonderful friend. Our researcher, Carleton English, is also amazing. We couldn't have done it without you.

HELAINE'S
ACKNOWLEDGMENTS

First, thank you to my cowriter, Harold Pollack, who invited me along on the wonderful journey that is *The Index Card*. As always, a huge thank-you to all the people who have shared their financial stories and expertise with me over the years. My friends also deserve a shout-out. I promise to host dinner parties again now that this is over—at least until I consider another book. A loving thank-you to my children, Jake and Luke, and parents, Carol and Nelson Olen, who kindly tolerate my book-writing habit. Finally, much is owed to my husband, Matt Roshkow, who combines the roles of spouse and in-house editor.

HAROLD'S ACKNOWLEDGMENTS

It goes without saying—but I will say it anyway—that I am very grateful to Helaine for her willingness to deploy her formidable financial and writing expertise in writing this book with me.

This project is a labor of love, to which I brought sometimes-embarrassing zeal. So I should start by asking forgiveness from many students, colleagues, friends, siblings, in-laws, step-siblings, and others who endured my essential—if oddly unsolicited—financial advice.

Eight years ago, Judith Levine came to my office with a statistics question. I don't remember if I answered the statistics question. I do remember haranguing her with semi-requested financial advice—advice that later became the index card. I am gratified that she admits to following it.

Many friends helped me in this effort. My blogging colleagues Mark Kleiman, Aaron Carroll, Austin Frakt, Mike

O'Hare, Keith Humphreys, Jonathan Cohn, Steve Anderson, and Chuck Smith-Dewey deserve special mention.

I am grateful to Ezra Klein, then my *Washington Post Wonkblog* editor, who called broad public attention to the index card. Joseph Weisenthal, Felix Salmon, and Penny Wang helped it go viral. I am gratified that two professional betters—Justin Wolfers and Sendhil Mullainathan—kindly noted it as well. My dissertation advisor, Richard Zeckhauser, offered much of the best financial and life advice, years before I thought to follow it.

Many Internet friends encouraged me in this project. Kathy Geier, Steve Teles, and Katha Pollitt were the first to suggest that the index card be made into a book. Henry Aaron, Dean Baker, David Boyum, Kevin Carey, Art Goldhammer, Burton Malkiel, Ben Miller, Rick Perlstein, and Rich Yeselson shared valuable knowledge. I benefited from train conversations with Josh Berg, Rick Eichmann, and Chris Lyttle. Robin Scott offered great encouragement, and Nick Epley deserves special mention for many valuable conversations along the way.

And of course, I want to thank my colleagues at the University of Chicago School of Social Service Administration for supporting me in so many ways.

My parents are surely relieved that I finally started listening to them about saving. My sister, Gail, and her husband, David, are wonderful role models of frugality. Cara and Bob, Dana, Cindy and Elio, and Liza and Mark were very supportive as well. My daughters, Rebecca and Hannah, and my brother-in-law Vincent have lived many of the personal anecdotes described in the book. All three hate my gleeful public references to our banged-up 2004 Sienna.

Most of all, my wife, Veronica, has been my partner in both the bitter and the sweet anecdotes that sprinkle this book.

NOTES

INTRODUCTION

4 **Almost three out of four of us:** American Psychological Association, "American Psychological Association Survey Shows Money Stress Weighing on Americans' Health Nationwide," February 4, 2015, http://www.apa.org/news/press/releases/2015/02/money-stress.aspx; Melanie Hicken, "Money Issues Are Still Really Stressing Americans Out," *CNN Money*, February 4, 2015, http://money.cnn.com/2015/02/04/pf/money-stress/.

4 **One-third of those in relationships:** American Psychological Association, *Stress in America: Paying with Our Health*, February 4, 2015, http://www.apa.org/news/press/releases/stress/2014/stress-report.pdf.

4 **Fifty-five percent of people:** Nanci Hellmich, "Many Americans Fear Going Broke in Retirement," *USA Today*, August 21, 2014, http://www.usatoday.com/story/money/personalfinance/2014/05/25/retirement-affluent-americans-going-broke/9383019/.

4 **Sixty-nine percent of us:** Statistics Brain Research Institute, "Percent of People Who Balance Their Checkbook," September 9, 2012, http://www.statisticbrain.com/percent-of-people-who-balance-their-checkbook/.

7 **"Veronica's brother Vincent"**: Veronica P. Pollack and Harold A. Pollack, "Bringing Vincent Home," *Health Affairs* 25, no. 1 (2006): 231–36.

11 **A life coach copied it:** Lucious Conway, "All of the Financial Advice You're Ever Going to Need Is Written on This Index Card," MyRecoveryCoach.biz, September 5, 2013, https://www.youtube.com/watch?v=1FaIJ-_32bs.

12 **"Pollack's right":** Ezra Klein, "This 4 × 6 Index Card Has All the Financial Advice You'll Ever Need," *Wonkblog* (blog), *Washington Post,* September 16, 2013, http://www.washingtonpost.com/blogs/wonkblog/wp/2013/09/16/this-4x6-index-card-has-all-the-financial-advice-youll-ever-need/.

12 **"Your new financial advisor":** Rob Beschizza, "Your New Financial Advisor Is Harold Pollack's Index Card," *Boing Boing,* September 17, 2013, http://boingboing.net/2013/09/17/your-new-financial-advisor-is.html.

12 *Marketplace, Forbes, the Huffington Post:* David Brancaccio, "Everything You Need to Know About Personal Finance—on One Index Card," *Marketplace,* September 17, 2013, http://www.marketplace.org/topics/economy/everything-you-need-know-about-personal-finance-one-index-card; Erik Carter, "All the Financial Advice You Need on an Index Card?," *Forbes,* January 1, 2015, http://www.forbes.com/sites/financialfinesse/2015/01/09/all-the-financial-advice-you-need-on-an-index-card/; "10 Amazing Pieces of Financial Advice Stuffed into 1 Cheat Sheet," *Huffington Post,* September 5, 2013, http://www.huffingtonpost.com/2013/09/05/financial-advice-_n_3874014.html; "An Index Card Made by Professor Harold Pollack,

Which Contains Just About All of the Financial Advice You're Ever Going to Need," *Reddit*, accessed June 4, 2015, http://www .reddit.com/r/pics/comments/2jqxon/an_index_card_made _by_professor_harold_pollack/; Thorin Klosowski, "All the Financial Investment Advice You'll Ever Need on One Index Card," *Lifehacker,* September 17, 2013, http://lifehacker.com/all -the-financial-advice-youll-ever-need-on-a-4x6-inde -1334131550.

12 **The MacArthur fellow:** Sendhil Mullainathan, "Want Financial Advice? 2) @haroldpollack Gives It Free . . . in Index Card Form," Twitter, September 4, 2013, https://twitter.com/m _sendhil/status/375421035127910400.

12 **So did top economists:** Justin Wolfers, "All the Financial Advice You Need, Summarized on @haroldpollack's Index Card," Twitter, September 4, 2013, https://twitter.com/justinwolfers /status/375431414462038016.

12 **Vanguard mentioned the index card:** John Woerth, "Vanguard's Index Card," *Vanguard Blog,* September 23, 2013, http://vanguardblog.com/2013/09/23/vanguards-index -card/.

12 *Money* **magazine called it:** "Best New Advice: Just What You Really Need," *Money,* December 2, 2013, http://time.com /money/2794936/best-new-ways-to-save-money/.

12 **"The most notable personal finance":** Lee Schafer, "Personal Finance Need Not Be Complicated," *Star Tribune,* December 29, 2013, http://www.startribune.com/business/237575981.html.

RULE #1

19 **Accounting for inflation:** U.S. Census Bureau, *Money Income in the United States, 1998,* September 1999, https://www.census .gov/prod/99pubs/p60-206.pdf.

19 **At the same time, income inequality:** Emmanuel Saez and Gabriel Zucman, "Wealth Inequality in the United States Since 1913: Evidence from Capitalized Income Tax Data" (NBER Working Paper 20625, 2014), http://www.nber.org/papers /w20625.

20 **According to economists Marianne Bertrand:** Marianne Bertrand and Adair Morse, "Trickle-Down Consumption" (NBER Working Paper 18883, 2013), http://www.nber.org/papers/w18883.

21 **A little more than a quarter:** U.S. Census Bureau, Wealth and Asset Ownership, Table 4, http://www.census.gov/people /wealth/files/Wealth_Tables_2011.xlsx.

21 **47 percent of us:** Board of Governors, Federal Reserve System, Report on the Economic Well-Being of U.S. Households in 2014, http://www.federalreserve.gov/econresdata/2014-report -economic-well-being-us-households-201505.pdf.

23 **According to Sendhil Mullainathan:** Sendhil Mullainathan and Eldar Shafir, *Scarcity: Why Having Too Little Means So Much* (New York: Times Books, 2013).

25 **According to a 2013 survey:** Dennis Jacobe, "One in Three Americans Prepare a Detailed Household Budget: Thirty Percent Prepare a Long-Term Financial Plan with Investment Goals," Gallup, June 3, 2013, http://www.gallup.com/poll/162872/one -three-americans-prepare-detailed-household-budget.aspx.

31 **That's the term trademarked:** David Bach, "Take the 'Start Over' Latte Factor® Challenge," accessed June 4, 2015, http://www.finishrich.com/lattefactor/.

32 **Do you really need to rent:** Jose Pagliery, "Comcast and Time Warner Cable Hike Modem Fees as Much as 33%. Time to Buy Your Own," *CNNMoney,* January 5, 2015, http://money.cnn.com/2015/01/02/technology/comcast-time-warner-cable-modem/.

33 **Make the time to better plan:** Dana Gunders, "Wasted: How America Is Losing Up to 40 Percent of Its Food from Farm to Fork to Landfill" (NRDC Issue Paper 12-06-B, 2012), http://www.nrdc.org/food/files/wasted-food-ip.pdf.

33 **According to a group of researchers:** Manoj Thomas, Kalpesh Kaushik Desai, and Satheeshkumar Seenivasan, "How Credit Card Payments Increase Unhealthy Food Purchases: Visceral Regulation of Vices," *Journal of Consumer Research* 38, no. 1 (2010): 126–39.

34 **"I remember standing over":** Terri Trespicio, "What Happened When I Spent One Month Living on Cash," *TueNight,* April 15, 2014, http://tuenight.com/2014/04/what-happened-when-i-spent-one-month-living-on-cash/.

36 **A few years ago, ING Direct:** Jennifer Saranow Schultz, "Multiple Savings Accounts, Multiple Goals," *Bucks* (blog), *New York Times,* July 1, 2010, http://bucks.blogs.nytimes.com/2010/07/01/multiple-savings-accounts-multiple-goals/.

RULE #2

42 **They weren't among the third of households:** Marilyn Geewax, "Chances Are Pretty Good That's a Bill Collector Calling," NPR,

July 29, 2014, http://www.npr.org/blogs/thetwo-way/2014/07/29
/336322389/chances-are-pretty-good-that-s-a-bill
-collector-calling.

42–43 **Average credit card debt:** Tim Chen, "American Household
Credit Card Debt Statistics: 2015," *Nerd Wallet,* http://www
.nerdwallet.com/blog/credit-card-data/average-credit-card
-debt-household/.

45 **Well, the real money for credit card issuers:** Sumit Agarwal,
Souphala Chomsisengphet, Neale Mahoney, and Johannes
Stroebel, "Regulating Consumer Financial Products: Evidence
from Credit Cards," *Quarterly Journal of Economics* 130, no. 1
(2015): 111–16.

46 **The average interest rate:** Kelly Dilworth, "Credit Card Interest
Rates Slide to 14.89 Percent," CreditCards.com, January 7, 2015,
http://www.creditcards.com/credit-card-news/interest-rate
-report-10715-down-2121.php.

47 **On store-branded cards, it is higher:** Paul Muschick, "Store
Credit Cards Have Perks, but Can Be Costly," *Morning
Call,* August 20, 2014, http://www.mcall.com/news/local
/watchdog/mc-store-credit-cards-watchdog-20140820-column
.html.

47 **According to economists Jialan Wang:** Jialan Wang and
Benjamin Keys, "Perverse Nudges: Minimum Payments and
Debt Paydown in Consumer Credit Cards," Society for
Economic Dynamics (2014 Meeting Papers), http://econpapers
.repec.org/paper/redsed014/323.htm.

52 **A study published in 2012:** Martha C. White, "The Verdict Is
In: Tackle Smaller Debts First," *Time.com,* August 16, 2012,

http://business.time.com/2012/08/16/the-verdict-is-in-tackle
-smaller-debts-first/.

55 **According to the *Wall Street Journal:*** AnnaMaria Andriotis,
"Credit-Card Comparison Sites Come Under Fire: Once-Close
Relationship Between Card Issuers and Websites Turns Frosty,"
Wall Street Journal, August 22, 2014.

56 **People's monthly spending on these cards:** Sumit Agarwal,
Sujit Chakravorti, and Anna Lunn, "Why Do Banks Reward
Their Customers to Use Their Credit Cards?" (WP 2010-19,
2010), http://www.chicagofed.org/digital_assets/publications
/working_papers/2010/wp2010_19.pdf.

59 ***There were about 900,000:*** Charles M. Oellermann and Mark G.
Douglas, "The Year in Bankruptcy 2013," Lexology, January 22,
2014, http://www.lexology.com/library
/detail.aspx?g=f3e7690b-6026-4a5c-8579-08253ba88d5f. See also
Robin Goldwyn Blumenthal, "An Era of Solvency: Bankruptcy
Bust?," *Barron's,* March 21, 2015, http://online.barrons.com/articles
/SB52018153252431963983004580522160895440490.

61 **The Federal Reserve estimates:** Board of Governors of the
Federal Reserve System, "Consumer Credit—G.19," statistical
release, March 2015, http://www.federalreserve.gov/releases/g19
/current/.

61 **A recent study published:** Beth Akers and Matthew M.
Chingos, "Are College Students Borrowing Blindly?" Brookings,
December 10, 2014, http://www.brookings.edu/research/reports
/2014/12/10-borrowing-blindly-akers-chingos.

64 **According to a report issued:** Deanne Loonin and Jillian
McLaughlin, *Searching for Relief: Desperate Borrowers and the*

Growing Student Loan "Debt Relief" Industry (National Consumer Law Center, 2013), https://www.nclc.org/issues /searching-for-relief.html.

RULE #3

69 **As for Social Security:** Monique Morrissey, "The Top 10 Myths About Social Security," *Working Economics Blog,* Economic Policy Institute, August 13, 2014, http://www.epi.org/blog /top-10-myths-social-security/.

70 **On average, Americans who reach:** Centers for Disease Control, "Table 22. Life Expectancy at Birth, at Age 65, and at Age 75, by Sex, Race, and Hispanic Origin: United States, Selected Years, 1900–2010" (2011), http://www.cdc.gov/nchs /data/hus/2011/022.pdf.

70 **More than a quarter of sixty-five-year-olds:** Elizabeth Arias, "United States Life Tables, 2010," *National Vital Statistics Reports* 63, no. 7 (2011), http://www.cdc.gov/nchs/data/nvsr /nvsr63/nvsr63_07.pdf.

72 **In fact, a majority of retirees:** Glenn Ruffenach, "Think You'll Work in Retirement? Think Again," Market Watch, June 2, 2015, http://www.marketwatch.com/story/think-youll-work-in -retirement-think-again-2015-06-02.

87 **A researcher for the Pension Policy Center:** Mark Miller, "Thinking of a Retirement Account Rollover? Think Twice," Reuters, December 23, 2014, http://www.reuters.com /article/2014/12/23/us-column-miller-retirement

-idUSKBN0K110020141223?feedType=RSS&feedName=
everything&virtualBrandChannel=11563.

87 **called a Coverdell Education Savings Account:** Internal
Revenue Service, Coverdell Education Savings Account (ESA),
Publication 970, chap. 7 (2014), www.irs.gov/publications/p970
/ch07.html.

87 **called a 529 plan:** Internal Revenue Service, "529 Plans:
Questions and Answers," accessed June 4, 2015, http://www.irs
.gov/uac/529-Plans:-Questions-and-Answers.

88 **Must generally be used before age thirty:** Finaid, "Coverdell
Education Savings Accounts" (n.d.), http://www.finaid.org
/savings/coverdell.phtml.

88 **"Some state plans impose age restrictions:** "529 Plans vs.
Coverdell Education Savings Accounts," 360 Degrees of
Financial Literacy, accessed June 4, 2015, http://
www.360financialliteracy.org/Topics/Paying-for-Education
/College-Savings-Options/529-Plans-vs.-Coverdell-Education
-Savings-Accounts.

89 **Many states provide:** Finaid, "State Tax Deductions for 529
Contributions" (2015), http://www.finaid.org/savings
/state529deductions.phtml.

89 **Account holder pays tax:** Internal Revenue Service, Coverdell
Education Savings Account (2014), http://www.irs.gov
/publications/p970/ch07.html—en_US_2014_publink1000178471.

RULE #4

92 **Kodak was so iconic:** Greg McFarlane, "The Fall from Glory:
Delisting Brands," *Investopedia,* February 6, 2012, http://www

.investopedia.com/financial-edge/0212/the-fall-from-glory
-delisting-brands.aspx.

96 **Their papers demonstrate:** Brad M. Barber and Terrance
Odean, "Trading Is Hazardous to Your Wealth: The Common
Stock Investment Performance of Individual Investors," *Journal
of Finance* 55, no. 2 (2000): 773–806.

98–99 **"Trying to pick a winning":** Felix Salmon, personal e-mail to
Harold Pollack.

99 **If anything, their overconfidence:** Daniel Kahneman, "Don't
Blink! The Hazards of Confidence," *New York Times Magazine,*
October 19, 2011.

99 **One other thing we learn:** Robert Carden, "Behavioral
Economics Show That Women Tend to Make Better Investments
Than Men," *Washington Post,* October 11, 2013, http://www
.washingtonpost.com/business/behavioral-economics
-show-that-women-tend-to-make-better-investments-than-men
/2013/10/10/5347f40e-2d50-11e3-97a3-ff2758228523_story.html.

100 **In its gentle way:** Jess Beltz and Robert Jennings, "'Wall Street
Week with Louis Rukeyser' Recommendations: Trading Activity
and Performance," *Review of Financial Economics* 6 (1997): 15–27.

101 **One academic analysis:** Bill Alpert, "Cramer's Star Outshines
His Stock Picks: Stock Picks Featured on *Mad Money* Don't Live
Up to the Host's Hype," *Barron's,* February 9, 2009.

RULE #5

114 **"How could a luminous protein":** Alan Fregtman, "T. Rowe
Price—Glass Jellyfish Spot," https://vimeo.com/25579208.

114 **According to a recent survey:** Larry Swedroe, "Here's the Latest Failing Grade for Active Funds," *MoneyWatch,* CBS, September 16, 2014, http://www.cbsnews.com/news/s-p-spiva-midyear-2014 -active-versus-passive-scorecard-active-underperforms-again/.

115 **A recent *New York Times* article:** Jeff Sommer, "Who Routinely Trounces the Stock Market? Try 2 out of 2,862 Funds," *New York Times,* July 19, 2014, http://www.nytimes.com/2014/07/20 /your-money/who-routinely-trounces-the-stock-market-try-2-out -of-2862-funds.html?_r=0.

116 **"A very low-cost S&P 500 index fund":** Mitch Tuchman, "Warren Buffett to Heirs: Put My Estate in Index Funds," *Retire Mentors,* March 13, 2014, http://www.marketwatch.com /story/warren-buffett-to-heirs-put-my-estate-in-index-funds -2014-03-13.

117 **As a result, while the average annual fee:** Investment Company Institute, *2014 Investment Company Fact Book* (2014), http:// www.icifactbook.org/pdf/2014_factbook.pdf.

118–119 **Robert Hiltonsmith, a researcher:** Robert Hiltonsmith, *The Retirement Savings Drain: The Hidden and Excessive Costs of 401(k)s* (Demos, 2012).

119 **It has a lovely and low:** "Vanguard 500 Index Fund Investor Shares (VFINX)," Vanguard, accessed June 4, 2015, https:// personal.vanguard.com/us/funds/snapshot?FundId=0040& FundIntExt=INT.

124 **On six occasions since 1997:** "List of Largest Daily Changes in the Dow Jones Industrial Average," *Wikipedia,* accessed June 4, 2015, http://en.wikipedia.org/wiki/List_of_largest_daily _changes_in_the_Dow_Jones_Industrial_Average.

125 **Since 1928, the S&P stock index:** Aswath Damodaran, "Historical Returns: Stocks, T.Bonds & T.Bills with Premiums," New York University, January 6, 2015.

128 **In fact, in 2013, Goldman Sachs:** Dan Strumpf, "Goldman: Global Slowdown to Take Bite out of S&P 500 Earnings," *Wall Street Journal,* October 30, 2014, http://blogs.wsj.com/moneybeat /2014/10/30/goldman-global-slowdown-to-take-bite-out-of-sp -500-earnings/.

RULE #6

134 **Eighty-seven percent of us:** S. Kathi Brown, *Fiduciary Duty and Investment Advice: Attitudes of 401(k) and 403(b) Recipients,* AARP, September 2013, http://www.aarp.org/content/dam/aarp /research/surveys_statistics/general/2013/Fiduciary-Duty -and-Investment-Advice-Attitudes-of-401k-and-403b -Participants-Executive-Summary-AARP-rsa-gen.pdf.

134 **Seventy-six percent of us:** Alexis Leondis, "Brokers Are Fiduciaries, Survey Says," *Bloomberg Business,* September 15, 2010, http://www.bloomberg.com/news/articles/2010-09-15 /-clueless-u-s-investors-believe-brokers-have-fiduciary-duty -survey-says.

134 **Sixty percent of us:** Mark Schoeff Jr., "Most Investors Think Brokers Are Fiduciaries, Survey Says," *Investment News,* September 15, 2010, http://www.investmentnews.com/article /20100915/FREE/100919956/most-investors-think-brokers-are -fiduciaries-survey-says.

136 **The best way to describe this standard:** Fi360-Advisor One, "Trustworthy Advice: Is the Fiduciary Standard the New

Normal for Financial Advisors? Findings of the 2012 fi360
-AdvisorOne Fiduciary Survey" (2012), http://www.fi360.com
/main/pdf/fiduciarysurvey_resultsreport_2012.pdf.

137 **At last count:** Jason Zweig and Mary Pilon, "Is Your Advisor
Pumping Up His Credentials? Those Fancy Initials After Your
Financial Advisor's Name Might Not Be as Impressive as They
Seem," *Wall Street Journal*, October 16, 2010, http://online.wsj.com
/articles/SB10001424052748703927504575540582361440848.

138 **Something called an accredited retirement advisor:** Consumer
Finance Protection Bureau, *Senior Designations for Financial
Advisors: Reducing Consumer Confusion and Risks,* April 18,
2013, http://files.consumerfinance.gov/f/201304_CFPB
_OlderAmericans_Report.pdf.

139 **These events are ridiculously common:** Lona Choi-Allum,
Protecting Older Investors: 2009 Free Lunch Seminar Report,
AARP, November 2009, http://assets.aarp.org/rgcenter/
consume/freelunch.pdf.

139 **That doesn't count the 13 percent:** Securities and Exchange
Commission, *Report of Examinations of Securities Firms
Providing "Free Lunch" Sales Seminars,* September 2007,
http://www.sec.gov/spotlight/seniors/freelunchreport.pdf.

141 **A recent survey published:** Nathaniel Popper, "Wall Street
Banks' Mutual Funds Can Lag on Returns," *New York Times,*
April 12, 2015, http://www.nytimes.com/2015/04/13/business/
dealbook/wall-street-banks-mutual-funds-can-lag-on-returns
.html.

142 **This is where Helaine likes to cite:** Sendhil Mullainathan,
Markus Noeth, and Antoinette Schoar, "The Market for

Financial Advice: An Audit Study" (NBER Working Paper 17929, 2012), http://www.nber.org/papers/w17929.

143 **Lest you think this is only an American problem:** Stephen Foerster, Juhani T. Linnainmaa, Brian T. Melzer, and Alessandro Previtero, "Retail Financial Advice: Does One Size Fit All?" (NBER Working Paper 20712, 2014), http://www.nber .org/papers/w20712.

145 **According to a 2011 survey:** Jennifer Johnson, "What Americans Don't Know about Financial Fees," *Fiscal Times,* December 4, 2012, http://www.thefiscaltimes.com/Articles /2012/12/04/What-Americans-Dont-Know-about-Financial-Fees.

146 **Altogether, the Obama administration:** "Fact Sheet: Middle Class Economics: Strengthening Retirement Security by Cracking Down on Backdoor Payments and Hidden Fees," White House press release, February 23, 2015, https://www .whitehouse.gov/the-press-office/2015/02/23/fact-sheet-middle -class-economics-strengthening-retirement-security-crac.

150 **As the fine print on brokerage forms indicates:** Fidelity, "Guide to Brokerage and Investment Advisory Services at Fidelity Investments," accessed June 4, 2015, http://personal.fidelity .com/accounts/services/BD-IA-Dscls.pdf.

151 **She suggests one put together:** Committee for the Fiduciary Standard, "Putting Your Interests First," accessed June 4, 2015, http://www.fi360.com/main/pdf/fiduciaryoath_individual.pdf.

RULE #7

157 **"Perhaps for the first time ever":** Glenn Altschuler and Stuart Blumin, *The GI Bill: The New Deal for Veterans* (New York:

Oxford University Press, 2009); Vincent J. Cannato, "A Home of One's Own," *National Affairs,* no. 3 (Spring 2010), http://www .nationalaffairs.com/publications/detail/a-home-of-ones -own.

158 **Even after the Great Recession's housing bust:** Rebecca Riffkin, "Americans Sold on Real Estate as Best Long-Term Investment: Lower-Income Americans Prefer Gold to Stocks, Savings Accounts, Bonds," Gallup, April 17, 2014, http://www.gallup .com/poll/168554/americans-sold-real-estate-best-long-term -investment.aspx.

158 **According to the February 2015 National Housing Survey:** FannieMae, "February 2015 Data Release," February 2015, http://www.fanniemae.com/resources/file/research /housingsurvey/pdf/nhs-monthly-data-030915.pdf.

158 **The National Association of Home Builders claims:** Michael Neal, "Homeownership Remains a Key Component of Household Wealth: September Special Study for Housing Economics," National Association of Home Builders, accessed June 4, 2015, http://www.nahb.org/fileUpload_details.aspx ?contentTypeID=3&contentID=215073&subContentID= 533787&channelID=311—42%%20of%20net%20wealth.

162 **According to Nobel Prize–winning economist:** Robert J. Shiller, *Irrational Exuberance,* 3rd ed. (Princeton, N.J.: Princeton University Press, 2015).

163 **Currently, half of renters:** Krishna Rao, "The Rent Is Too Damn High," April 15, 2014, http://www.zillow.com/research/rent -affordability-2013q4-6681/; Shaila Dewan, "In Many Cities, Rent Is Rising Out of Reach of Middle Class," *New York Times,* April

14, 2014, http://www.nytimes.com/2014/04/15/business/more
-renters-find-30-affordability-ratio-unattainable.html.

173 **According to the Consumer Financial Protection Bureau:**
Sergei Kulaev, "Nearly Half of Mortgage Borrowers Don't Shop
Around When They Buy a Home," CFPB, January 13, 2015,
http://www.consumerfinance.gov/blog/nearly-half-of-mortgage
-borrowers-dont-shop-around-when-they-buy-a-home/.

RULE #8

179–180 **The annual Mom Salary Survey:** "Salary.com's 14th Annual
Mom Salary Survey," Salary.com, http://www.salary.com
/mom-paycheck/.

182 **Married couples need to amass:** Chye-Ching Huang and
Brandon Debot, "Ten Facts You Should Know About the Federal
Estate Tax," Center on Budget and Policy Priorities, March 23,
2015, http://www.cbpp.org/cms/?fa=view&id=2655.

184 **The average monthly payment is rather low:** Social Security
Administration, "Social Security: Monthly Statistical Snapshot,
March 2015," March 2015, http://www.ssa.gov/policy/docs
/quickfacts/stat_snapshot/2015-03.pdf, see Table 2.

184 **The majority of applications:** United States Social Security
Administration, *Annual Statistical Report on the Social Security
Disability Insurance Program, 2011.* Outcomes of Applications
for Disability Benefits, Chart 11, http://www.ssa.gov/policy
/docs/statcomps/di_asr/2011/sect04.html#chart11.

187 **How much you will save:** Kimberly Lankford, "An Easy Way to
Save on Homeowners Insurance," *Kiplinger's,* July 30, 2013,

http://www.kiplinger.com/article/insurance/T028-C001
-S001-an-easy-way-to-save-on-homeowners-insurance
.html.

187 **According to one survey:** Krystal Steinmetz, "Money Talks
News: Here's How Much You'll Save by Raising Your Car
Insurance Deductible from $500 to $1,000," *Yahoo! Finance,*
October 6, 2014, http://finance.yahoo.com/news/much-ll-save
-raising-car-001040665.html.

188 **The cheapest 2015 Toyota Sienna:** Bengt Halvorson, "2015
Toyota Sienna—Review," The Car Connection, March 25, 2015,
http://www.thecarconnection.com/overview/toyota_sienna
_2015; Toyota USA Newsroom. "Toyota Announces Pricing for
New 2015 Sienna Minivan," September 2, 2014, http://
toyotanews.pressroom.toyota.com/releases/2015+toyota+
sienna+pricing.htm.

192 **According to the management consultancy Aon Hewitt:** "Aon
Hewitt Analysis Shows Upward Trend in U.S. Health Care Cost
Increases," Aon Hewitt, November 13, 2014, http://ir.aon.com
/about-aon/investor-relations/investor-news/news-release
-details/2014/Aon-Hewitt-Analysis-Shows-Upward
-Trend-in-US-Health-Care-Cost-Increases/default.aspx.

197 **Yes, we're looking at you, Gerber:** Libby Kane, "Here's Why
Your Child Probably Doesn't Need Life Insurance," Business
Insider, June 4, 2014, http://www.businessinsider.com
/do-children-need-life-insurance-2014-6.

198 **In the aftermath of Hurricane Sandy:** David W. Chen, "FEMA
to Review All Flood Damage Claims from Hurricane Sandy,"
New York Times, March 12, 2015, http://www.nytimes.com

/2015/03/13/nyregion/fema-to-review-hurricane-sandy-flood
-claims-amid-scandal-over-altered-reports.html.

198 **In the case of health insurance:** Jones Day, *The Affordable Care
Act at 2½—What Employers Should Expect Now* (Jones Day
White Paper, August 2012), http://www.jonesday.com/files
/Publication/19616e5b-8d4b-428e-b0f4-35130e029814
/Presentation/PublicationAttachment/549ba7a4-042b-45a2
-bf7f-3bca509c04d2/Affordable Care Act.pdf.

RULE #9

205 **When Mettler ran surveys:** Suzanne Mettler, *The Submerged
State* (Chicago: University of Chicago Press, 2011).

INDEX

Note: Page numbers in *italics* refer to charts or graphs.

All the Financial Advice You'll Ever Need on One Card

Rule #1: Strive to Save 10 to 20 Percent of Your Income

Rule #2: Pay Your Credit Card Balance in Full Every Month

Rule #3: Max Out Your 401(K) and Other Tax-Advantaged Savings Accounts

Rule #4: Never Buy or Sell Individual Stocks

Rule #5: Buy Inexpensive, Well-Diversified Indexed Mutual Funds and Exchange-Traded Funds

Rule #6: Make Your Financial Advisor Commit to the Fiduciary Standard

Rule #7: Buy a Home When You Are Financially Ready

Rule #8: Insurance—Make Sure You're Protected

Rule #9: Do What You Can to Support the Social Safety Net

Rule #10: Remember the Index Card